THE GUIDE TO SUCCESS IN YOUR CAREER:

BECOME THE BOSS WOMAN YOU ARE MEANT TO BE

Lindsey Brookes

Building Your Successful Career.

Introduction
  Command the Room

Brand You

Be Brave and Get Out of Your Comfort Zone

Identify with a Successful Image

Get Rid of Self-Doubt

Build Influence

Always Find New Opportunities to Learn

Lead with Power
    Women want to return to work.

  Country Options
    Australia
    United States
    United Kingdom
    Canada
    New Zealand

  A short discussion on returning to work after divorce

Why Women Return to Work
  Benefits of working outside the home

  History

  Why are women going back to work today?

  Money is the primary motivation

How do you begin the Switching industries?
  Making a goal

  Additional brainstorming

  Begin with a list about your job experience or interests

  The steps to the goal

  The action plan

  Now, let's fill in some of the stones:

Daily plan

More on goals

Why goals don't work

How to help succeed with your goals

Checklist
　Goals
　Considerations and compromises

The Corporate World

Changing Careers

What to consider when making a career change

Working out of home

A few considerations for working out of home

Checklist

Telecommuting

Other work-at-home ideas

Franchises

Business Opportunities

Social Media Marketing/Influencer

Web-based Businesses

Working for yourself

Starting your own business

Some of the steps involved

Considerations in working for yourself

Gaining Self-Confidence

　Developing confidence

　Recognize that you don't have to do it alone

　Accept that you are human

　Mistakes happen: keep moving

　Celebrate successes

- Some additional points
- Tools of a confident person
- Stay on task
- Know that you can do it
- Patience
- Choose your battles
- Other traits
- A few advanced skills
- Ways to network
- Checklist

What to wear in the workplace
- A little about what clothes say about you
- Dressing for the workplace
- Dress for your audience
- What is inappropriate?
- Other situations
- The difference between business casual and formal
- Casual Fridays
- A few more situations
- Dressing for the interview
- Dress for networking
- Dress for company functions
- Dress for your own business
- Summary on dressing for the job
- Checklist

Supporting yourself
- Ways to support yourself
- Exercise

- Eat and sleep
- A life of lists
- Dealing with stress
- Fun
- A few more ideas
- Checklist

Organizing yourself

- Integrating Techniques
- Establish a routine
- Morning
- Several follow-up thoughts
- Hire a Personal assistant
- Planning meals
- Additional considerations around meals
- A few final ideas
- Checklist

Prepare

Panel

Introduction

Command the Room

Body Language

It's often said that communication is 55 percent body language, 38 percent tone of voice, and only 7 percent spoken a word, but these figures come from research carried out by Albert Mehrabian in the early 1970s that was never intended to be used as a hard-and-fast rule in every situation. Today, however, experts generally agree that approximately 60 percent of daily communication is verbal and the remaining 40 percent is nonverbal, including body language and tone of voice. Allan and Barbara Pease, the authors of The Definitive Book of Body Language, believe that, in a business environment, 60–80 percent of the impact made in a meeting or around a negotiating table comes down to body language. We use words to say what we want others to hear, but it's the tone of voice and body language we use as we speak that helps to convey deeper meaning and intent. The authors also believe that women are better than men at reading body language, and research carried out by psychologists at Harvard University has demonstrated that "women's intuition" is an innate skill, making women more perceptive of nonverbal cues.

The American actress Mae West once said, "I speak two languages: Body and English." In the 1930s, her fame as an actress, comedian, singer, screenwriter, and playwright was growing, and she certainly knew how to command a room. Her posture, attitude, and tone of voice all helped to convey her Hollywood star status, but commanding a room is not about making a big noise—it's about learning how to use verbal and nonverbal communication to project a professional image and convey status in any environment, including the workplace.

Confident women command a room by ...

Making eye contact with and acknowledging other people in the room. To command a room, others in the room need to know you're there. If you enter quietly without saying a word, your presence in the room may go completely unnoticed. It's not about being loud and drawing attention to yourself in a potentially negative way; simply acknowledge others with a smile, a nod of your head, or a wave of your hand when appropriate. When you acknowledge others, they, in turn, acknowledge you, but you also make them feel important, which helps to foster mutual respect.

Positioning themselves to be seen and to see others. Where you sit in a room is important. If you position yourself in a quiet corner or on the sidelines, you instantly present yourself as being less important than others in the room. To command the room, you need to sit where you can be seen by others and where you can engage with others. You're not there to make up the numbers; you're there to take part in the proceedings, so choose a central position. Facebook COO Sheryl Sandberg puts it this way: "Don't expect that you'll get to the corner office by sitting on the sidelines. Women need to sit at the table."

Using their posture, attitude, and tone of voice to make their presence known. Again, it's not about making a big noise, it's about making a positive impact. Confident women sit or stand with a confident posture, occupying their space in the room and using open body language to invite others to engage with them rather than closing themselves off with a guarded posture such as folded arms. They actively contribute to discussions and conversations without asking for permission to interject, especially when they have expert knowledge on a topic, and they never apologize for having something to say.

Social psychologist Amy Cuddy believes that open, expansive postures such as standing with your hands on your hips (think Wonder Woman) or sitting with your arms up and hands laced behind your head create the impression of being bigger, thereby creating a bigger presence in a room. The key finding in her research into body language and power is that adopting expansive postures makes us feel more powerful, more confident, and more assertive, and we are therefore perceived as being more powerful by others. This feeling of power also makes us speak more slowly. We're in control of what we say and how we say it, so we effectively expand the speaking space we have, which helps us to share ideas more openly. She says, "When we feel powerful, we expand. When we feel powerless, we shrink."

Listening to others.

Being able to listen is an important communication skill, and giving others your undivided attention when they speak is the only way to encourage them to extend the same courtesy to you. If you show any interest in others, they will show an interest in you, but learning how to command a room comes down to knowing when to speak and when to listen—letting your body language do the talking for you.

Commanding with charisma.

Mae West had charismatic charm, as did Marilyn Monroe and Princess Diana. They all shared an ability to express themselves through body language and to command attention without saying a word, but charismatic people don't hog the limelight, they are skilled at letting other people know they matter.

If you want to command a room, what you say is important. No one is going to listen if you have nothing relevant or of interest to say, but getting your message across requires a confident delivery. Remember, "A strong, confident person can rule the room with knowledge, personal style, attitude, and great posture." Nonverbal communication is equally important.

TRY THIS

Begin by making a study of your own body language. The way you feel comes across in your body language. Most of your gestures and movements will be subconscious, so become more aware of the body language you use. You already know how you feel, so begin to make connections between your commonly used body language and your emotions. For example, pay attention to what you do with your hands when you're in a meeting and note whether you cross your legs or fold your arms.

Next, study inspirational role models. Take a look at the people you admire. What messages do they communicate through their body language? Watch them in action. Observe their posture, their facial expressions, and their hand gestures—everything that helps them to come across as the person you admire.

Then, make notes and compare. What do women who command a room do differently to you? Knowledge is power. Use what you learn to begin developing your own effective body language through mirroring their example, taking care not to get too caught up in observing others as it's important to create your own style.

And finally, to build your confidence as you learn to use more open, expansive body language, try power posing. Amy Cuddy believes that adopting a powerful pose such as standing tall with feet apart and hands on hips for two minutes can give your confidence a powerful boost. She recommends standing in this expansive posture for two minutes before taking part in any event that requires you to feel and be seen as confident, powerful, and assertive.

Use the steepling gesture. In his studies of body movements, the anthropologist Ray Birdwhistell found that powerful politicians, lawyers, and executives gave instructions while using this power position. You can achieve this position by separating your palms slightly with fingertips lightly touching each other to making a little rooftop, like the steeple on a building. This is how this hand position looks like.

What You Say: What Leadership and Confidence Sounds Like

Don't pose your statements as questions! Minimize your "upspeak." Women's voices sometimes rise at the end of a sentence as if they're asking a question. Posing statements as questions makes you appear less confident and opens the door for people to dismiss your ideas.

Every time you find yourself presenting your ideas as questions, stop and change them into statements.

> Instead of saying, "Do you think we should ... ?" start saying, "I recommend us..." Leveling your voice through practice can, therefore, help you become more authoritative.

Brand You

"Do not desire to fit in. Desire to lead."—Mary Kay Ash

In 1999, Mary Kay Ash was awarded the title of Most Outstanding Woman in Business in the 20th Century by Lifetime Television. Today, she's considered America's greatest woman entrepreneur, but it all began back in 1963 when Mary Kay realized that she no longer desired to fit in; she dared to lead.

Mary Kay Cosmetics, Inc., was founded with an investment of $5,000 and a salesforce of only nine women. According to the latest figures, the company now has an estimated value of approximately $2.6 billion, and the number of independent beauty consultants selling Mary Kay products has grown to over 3.5 million operating in 35 global markets. Mary Kay Ash founded her company on a desire to lead and to forge a path for women to succeed in what she viewed to be a male-dominated business world.

Desire to Lead

Mary Kay the brand became a reflection of Mary Kay, the person. Your personal brand image must reflect your core values and beliefs, but all power women began building their brand on shared principles, and you can adopt and apply the same strategies to develop your own brand:

Take credit for your achievements. Unless you're prepared to showcase your skills and abilities in the workplace, your achievements may go completely unnoticed, or credit for them may be claimed by someone else. Get comfortable with taking full credit for your achievements and speak up when your efforts are being overlooked.

Don't be too modest. No one makes it to the top of their game on their own, and arrogance is not an attractive character trait, but it is possible to be too modest. If you're unwilling to take credit where it's due, you risk being seen by others as a follower rather than a leader. Actively seek opportunities to showcase your skills and speak up about your successes; otherwise, you may find yourself overlooked. If you don't believe in your abilities, who will?

Don't give away your ideas. Believe in your ideas in the same way you believe in yourself. Mary Kay put her name on her idea and turned it into a business that reflected her core values and beliefs. Her idea paved the way for millions of other women to succeed, but she didn't give it away.

Brand You

A brand is simply a recognizable name, design, or symbol that makes the thing it represents stand out from other things. It might be a product or a company, but either way, people buy into the brand because it represents what that product or company stands for—their brand is their reputation. When building a personal brand, you're building your own recognizable image that will make you stand out from the crowd and represents the value you offer in your field.

If you're an entrepreneur building a business, your target audience needs to know what your business is and what it can offer them. They also need to know what makes your offering different to your competition's offerings—what makes you a better choice for them? If you're looking for promotion in your current workplace or planning to move into a new career, the departments responsible for hiring new talent need to know who you are, what you can offer them, and what makes you the best choice for them. This is where a strong personal brand can help you to stand out as the person they need.

Strong Personal Brands

Power women have strong personal brands. No matter what their field, they all promote what they represent and what they do best through their brand, and they make those brands strong by being these three things:

1. Authentic

Angela Merkel is a perfect example of a woman who has cultivated a strong, authentic personal brand. She is currently at the top of Forbes's World's 100 Most Powerful Women list, but her personal brand is just as powerful as her political status. Her hardworking, practical, unglamorous image made her unpopular with some people early in her career, but instead of changing her image to suit her critics, she used it to promote her pragmatic, down-to-earth approach to leadership. Successful business brands are built on consistency, and it takes a consistent, authentic personal brand to build the same success.

2. Different

Successful women do things differently. Facebook COO Sheryl Sandberg offers a great example of taking something that already exists and making it your own by approaching it differently. With her call to lean in, she promoted women's leadership in her own unique way. She advised women to bring their whole selves to work, not just their public or professional persona, meaning they should drop the commonly held opinion that to get ahead in the workplace they would need to adopt a stereotypically "male" approach—being aggressive and never showing vulnerability. By boldly pointing out that women often hold themselves back in the workplace by not believing in themselves and their abilities as women and leaders, she did something that no other high-profile woman in business had done before her. Her personal brand has inspired many more women to follow her lead.

3. Visible

No matter how good your offering or how different your approach, no one is going to know about it unless you make yourself visible. A strong business brand is a recognized brand, and a strong personal brand makes you stand out. During her years at Google, Marissa Mayer became the public face of the company. She rose through the ranks, creating a strong personal brand as an "articulate geek," giving her a unique edge.

TRY THIS

In the business world, companies need a strong brand to stand out from the crowd. The same principles can be applied to creating your own personal brand. Brand You is who you are, what you have to offer, and what you stand for.

Begin by understanding who you are to understand your value. Sit down and write out a list of everything you're good at. What skills do you have? What tasks do you excel at? What unique experiences have helped shape your skills and expertise? What makes you different? You need to know what you have to offer to know what needs you can address and where you can offer the most value.

Next, know what you stand for. Put your core values into words. What drives your career ambitions? What matters most in business and in the workplace? What personal attributes do you value most? It's important that the person you believe yourself to match the person others believe you to be. Sticking to your values in your words and your actions makes you an authentic "brand" that can be trusted.

Then, be the best. When you know who you are, what you offer, and what you stand for, be the best in every aspect. Never stop striving to be a better you, both personally and professionally. Knowledge is power, so build your brand by building your knowledge and your self-confidence. Desire to lead, be the leader you want to be. Be bold, be different, and be visible by doing what you do better than anyone else. As Anita Roddick, founder of the Body Shop, once said, "If you do things well, do them better."

Be Brave and Get Out of Your Comfort Zone

Adjust Your Mind-set

Psychologist Carol Dweck is the author of Mindset: The New Psychology of Success, and after decades of research, she believes that adopting a growth mindset holds the key to achieving success in all areas of life. In a growth mindset, you believe that change is always possible and that you have unlimited potential to achieve more. In comparison, a fixed mindset keeps you stuck where you are, held back by the belief that your situation can't be changed.

In both her personal and business life, Sheryl Sandberg has struggled with self-doubt on many occasions. She knows that fear can keep you trapped in your comfort zone and prevent you from realizing your true potential, but she has learned to silence the voices of doubt in her mind by asking herself, "What would I do if I weren't afraid?" In doing so, she has learned to adopt a growth mindset. Power women push themselves to achieve more by consistently stepping out of their comfort zones. They all have a growth mindset, so the key to achieving your own success lies in learning to do the same.

TRY THIS

Be brave and step out of your comfort zone by learning how to adopt a growth mindset.

Learn to hear your fixed mindset, "voice." In a fixed mindset, your inner voice of self-doubt may be saying, "You're not good enough to do this," or "Don't even try it, you'll only mess up."

Recognize that you have a choice. The way you interpret a challenging situation is entirely your choice. Recognize that the negative voice in your head doesn't have all the answers, and you don't need to listen to it.

Talkback with a growth mindset voice. Your fixed mindset voice may be asking, "What if you fail?" but you can reply with a growth mindset voice and say, "What if I succeed?" Tell yourself that most successful people experienced failures along the way, and choose to focus on the potential for success.

Take the growth mindset action. The process of learning to override the fixed mindset voice and drown it out with a growth mindset voice will take time, but the choice of how to deal with challenges and setbacks is ultimately yours to make. Take control.

Identify with a Successful Image

"People seldom improve when they have no other model but themselves to copy." —Oliver Goldsmith

When successful women are asked if they have a role model or image they identify with, the answer is always "yes." In recent interviews, Oprah Winfrey named Maya Angelou as a role model, Oscar nominee Jessica Chastain named fellow actress Isabelle Huppert, and Michelle Obama named Eleanor Roosevelt. But when they were asked to give reasons for their choices, it became clear that even though these role models have found success in their chosen careers, that's not what makes them ideal role models—it's their attitude.

Do We Need Role Models?

A good role model is someone you can look up to, someone with values you admire, someone whose thoughts and actions you want to emulate—someone you think of when facing a challenging situation, asking yourself, "What would they do?" We do need role models, but the aim must always be to find a role model who inspires us to become better versions of ourselves—the best we can possibly be.

A positive role model can act as a guide, helping you to understand the actions you can take to become the person you want to be and the attitude you need to adopt to achieve your goals. This means that the ideal role model for you is someone who possesses the character traits you will need to get you from where you are now to where you want to be.

Becoming Your Best Self

People seldom improve when they have no other model but themselves to copy. The role models chosen by the successful women listed above all have character traits and attitudes they admire and aspire to emulate—not so that they can become carbon copies of those individuals, but rather better versions of themselves.

Those traits include:

Optimism

Confidence

Passion

Humility

Integrity

Tenacity

- **Respect**

Oprah Winfrey admired Maya Angelou's positive outlook on life and lifelong zeal for learning. Jessica Chastain admired Isabelle Huppert's willingness to step out of her comfort zone and try new things. Michelle Obama admired Eleanor Roosevelt's forthright attitude and determination to push boundaries by speaking up for those struggling to make their voices heard. Becoming your best self is all about identifying the characteristics and attitudes you will need to achieve your goals, and then learning through the example of others who possess those attributes.

The Ripple of Influence

Identifying with a role model is not about trying to achieve their success; it's about getting into their mind and discovering the everyday thought processes, actions, and habits that have allowed them to succeed, and developing the same attitudes to pursue your own success.

Dame Kelly Holmes is a role model for many aspiring athletes. They might follow her training program, her diet plan, and wear her chosen brand of sports clothing, but unless they understand the thoughts and beliefs that drive her actions and the strengths in her character that allow her to overcome setbacks and injury, their dream of matching her Olympic success is unlikely to become their reality. Dame Kelly is an inspirational role model, but it takes an understanding of her mental strengths as well as her physical strengths to understand what is required to achieve Olympic gold.

Role models inspire the success of others, but those role models also have role models, and those they inspire may go on to become role models themselves. In the same way that a pebble dropped into a pond creates ripples that reach ever outwards, the ripple of influence can spread far and wide through an inspirational role model. It's not about being famous; it's all about demonstrating the character strengths that others aspire to call their own. Parents and relatives can be positive role models for children. Teachers and coaches can be positive role models for students, and friends and work colleagues can be role models for one another on many levels.

TRY THIS

Here are five things you can do today to identify with a successful image:

Ask yourself: What do you value most? Take time to consider the core values that guide your decisions in life and make you the person you are or want to be. Write them down.

Next, ask yourself: To live by these values and be the person you want to be every hour of every day, what character traits and attributes do you need to have? Write them down.

Look at your lists and identify people you know who already demonstrate those values and possess those traits. These may be people you know personally or people you admire from afar. It may not be possible to identify one person who offers the whole package, so create a list of people and note the attributes they have that make them a good role model for you.

Make a study of these individuals. Look beyond their success and accomplishments to learn as much as possible about their daily lives and routines. Observe them, read about them, listen to them talk. What beliefs, thoughts, and emotions drive their actions? What events have helped shape them into the people they are today? What motivates them on a day-to-day basis? How do they deal with setbacks? Who are their role models? How do they interact with other people in daily life?

Find ways to connect. Spending time with positive people is both inspirational and motivational. Find ways to spend time with and be around the positive role models you know or look for ways to connect through social media. The more you know about the people you admire, the more you learn about what makes them tick. Use what you learn to become a better you and to achieve your own success.

Get Rid of Self-Doubt

> "When you doubt your power, you give power to your doubt."—Honoré de Balzac

It's natural to experience self-doubt from time to time, but according to executive coach Janet Ioli, women are particularly prone to doubting themselves and their abilities at every stage in their careers—even when they make it all the way to the top. Many high achievers with solid track records of success continue to struggle with self-doubt. It can manifest as feelings of being unqualified for one's job or undeserving of praise or accolades, or as a fear of being "found out" as a fraud, and it's known as impostor syndrome.

Exercise Your Confidence Muscles

Poet and author Maya Angelou often spoke of feelings of inadequacy and of being "found out," actress Emma Watson has spoken in interviews about her experiences with crippling self-doubt and insecurity, and Facebook COO Sheryl Sandberg has spoken openly many times about her struggles with lacking self-confidence. "Confidence and leadership are muscles," she said. "You learn to use them or not to." What she means by this is that every time you do something that makes you uncomfortable, such as speaking up in a meeting or taking your place at the conference table rather than sitting on the sidelines, you exercise your confidence muscles and they will get stronger as a result. If you don't use them, just like the muscles in your body, they become weaker.

Alison Wagonfeld is Vice President of Marketing for Google Cloud. In her career, she's had to exercise her confidence muscles to help her deal with self-doubt in meetings. "In group discussions, like board meetings and investment team meetings, I try to speak up in the first 15 minutes," she says. "If I get involved in the conversation early, I feel more confident contributing throughout." She has also learned to be mindful of the language she uses, both spoken and written. "I'm sorry," is now a phrase she tries to avoid. She believes that apologizing puts her in a less confident state of mind, whether it's apologizing for speaking up at a meeting or beginning an email with an apology for not responding sooner.

Former vice president of Adobe Systems Karen Catlin turns to her V myth-busting posse" when she finds herself in the grips of imposter syndrome: "These are the people I can be vulnerable with, those I confide in when I lack confidence." Her myth-busting posse helps her to fend off insecurities by reminding her of her accomplishments and the reasons why her success is deserved.

Forgive Mistakes

Self-doubt leads many women to judge themselves harshly and set impossible, unrealistic expectations for themselves to achieve perfection in everything they do. Mistakes made are therefore considered to be confirmation of their inadequacy, creating an ongoing cycle of doubt and self-criticism.

Jessica Lawrence Quinn is the founder of NY Tech Meetup. She believes that the best way to deal with mistakes is to remember that everyone messes up at some point and that the mistakes you make don't define who you are. Mistakes are only failures if you fail to learn from them and take the positives forward with you as you move on. "Part of performing at your peak," she says, "is forgiving yourself when you're not—and moving on." This means adopting a growth mindset and accepting that a less-than-perfect performance today does not mean that you can't learn, adapt, improve, and do better tomorrow:

An unproductive day at your desk doesn't mean that you're a lazy, unproductive person; you can do more tomorrow.

A talk that doesn't go as planned or achieves the desired outcome doesn't mean that you're a poor speaker; you can learn and improve.

•One failure at closing a sale doesn't make you a failure as a salesperson.

Self-doubt and fear of failure go hand in hand. When you doubt your abilities, you fear stepping out of your comfort zone, so any failure experienced when you do step out will often spiral quickly into thoughts of giving up. This was something, Dona Sarkar, now a lead software engineer at Microsoft experienced in her first year at the University of Michigan. She had less coding experience than others in the computer science program, but she was reluctant to ask questions out of a fear of exposing her limited knowledge: "I was so afraid to go up and ask questions because one of the guys had made a comment about girls being airheads." Trying to muddle through on her own resulted in her failing the class, and Sarkar gave serious consideration to dropping out of the program completely. She talked herself out of it, however, and repeated the class, this time passing. "I told myself, this is my dream, and I'm not going to let one failure hold me back. ... I cried a bunch, said I'd never do it again, then I got back on two days later and did fine."

"Try something. Fail. And do it again."—Dona Sarkar

Celebrate Every Win

When thoughts of doubt are at the forefront of your mind, it's all too easy to focus only on failure and the things that don't quite go to plan.

In those moments, believing that things always go wrong for you or that you're not deserving of success gives power to your doubt.

Try This

To help deal with feelings of self-doubt, take the advice of experts and learn from the hands-on experiences of women who have found ways to take power away from their doubt.

Accentuate the positives: On an index card, write down the talents, strengths, and attributes you possess that have helped you to succeed. Keep the card with you and look at it whenever self-doubt creeps into your mind or whenever failure leaves you feeling like giving up.

Grow your own myth-busting posse: Follow Karen Catlin's advice and identify your own "myth-busting posse." These might be friends or relatives who know you well or work colleagues who know your strengths, talents, and abilities. Whenever you're having a confidence crisis, let their encouragement help silence the negative voices of doubt in your mind.

Start journaling: Expand on Sheryl Sandberg's habit of writing down three positive things at the end of each day by starting a journal. Scientific research has shown that developing a habit of positive journaling experiences helps to boost the release of feel-good endorphins because the writing process allows the events to be relived through memory. The self-esteem boost this creates can then be recalled whenever doubt creeps to the forefront of your mind.

Build Influence

"The key to successful leadership today is influence, not authority."—Ken Blanchard

To succeed in any field, you need influence. When you have influence, your point of view is listened to, and your ideas are considered worthy of attention. However, according to Kathryn Heath, coauthor of The Influence Effect, women in the workplace find it harder than men to build influence. "Studies show that imitating male characteristics doesn't translate to professional advancement for women," she says. "We women do not like unbridled competition, backroom deals, or trading favors. We favor collaboration, inclusion, and win-win outcomes. The distinctive missing link is an influence."

Begin Building

Krystal Covington is a marketing consultant with a special interest in workplace influence. Her research has uncovered three key areas around which influence can be built.

Presence. We've all heard the expressions "dress to impress" and "look the part," and in terms of building influence, the way you present yourself matters. However, creating a powerful presence goes beyond clothing to include body language and the way you interact with others. "Our presence is both the way we walk into a room and the clothes we wear on our bodies," Krystal says. "It's the first thing people judge when they see us and dictates a huge part of the impressions we make."

Reputation. To build a good reputation, you need to be credible. Gaining qualifications in your field are one way to boost credibility, but demonstrating relevant experience and ability is just as important. In Attitude 2, you learned the value of creating your own personal brand to stand out from the crowd, but your brand image can also help to grow your reputation, promoting who you are and what you stand for.

Visibility. In the same way that being visible is an essential element of building a personal brand, you need to get your ideas out there to be considered worthy of attention. The more visible and consistent you are in the way you present yourself and your ideas, the more trusted and influential you become.

The Power of Networking

It stands to reason that knowing a lot of people gives you greater power to influence simply because you have more people to share information with. Research in the field of power and influence has shown that networking can build influence, but doing so is dependent on building relationships with people within the network. Influencing someone you know will always be easier than influencing a stranger, and it's for this reason that social networks such as Facebook have been found less effective than face-to-face meetings in terms of building trust. Your power to influence depends on the strength of your network relationships, and the strength of those relationships will depend largely on the amount of time you've devoted to developing the three key areas of presence, reputation, and visibility.

An excellent example of the power of networking can be found in Christine Lagarde. She was the first woman to hold the position of finance minister in France, and she is the first to become managing director of the International Monetary Fund. Her experience gave her the credentials she needed to be considered for the role, but highly successful women proactively promote themselves through carefully planned marketing and networking campaigns; they leave nothing to chance. Christine used the power of networking across the globe to ensure she would have the support she needed to secure the position she wanted.

The greater your presence, reputation, and visibility, the greater your potential to influence others. People need to know who you are and what skills or expertise you have before they can judge your value as a network partner. There's also a great deal of truth in the saying, "It's not what you know, it's who you know," because the more powerful, influential people in your network and the more frequently you connect with them, the more opportunities you gain to build your reputation and influence through those connections.

Building Relationships to Build Influence

The connections you make can also help you to identify potential mentors. The right mentor for you will have the right mix of skills and experience to help you achieve your goals, but essential qualities include empathy, honesty, and superior communication skills. These qualities can only be identified by building personal relationships.

> "If I hadn't had mentors, I wouldn't be here today. I'm a product of great mentoring, great coaching. ... Coaches or mentors are very important." — Indra Nooyi, CEO, PepsiCo

Developing your communication skills enhances your ability to build meaningful relationships. The better your connection with people on a personal level, the greater your power to influence.

Celeste Headlee is a radio broadcaster who believes everyone can benefit from taking the time to hone their interpersonal conversational skills. In her popular TED Talk, she offers the following pointers.

Don't multitask. Give the person you're talking to your full attention.

Listen. Listening is a skill, and it is just as important as talking in terms of communication skills.

Go with the flow. Allow a conversation to take its course; it's not a script.

Use open-ended questions. Show genuine interest in others, and they'll show interest in you.

It's okay to say you don't know. Don't pretend to be an expert when you're not; authenticity is key to building trust.

With well-honed communication skills, you can make others feel important. Everyone likes to feel valued and accepted, and your influence goes a long way when others feel important in your presence.

TRY THIS

Build connections. Building influence begins with building connections. Dorie Clark, the author of Entrepreneurial You, says, "At a fundamental level, one of the reasons that people do things for you—support your idea, or approve your budget—is because they like you." Building connections is all about building rapport with your colleagues and the people you interact with regularly.

Develop expertise. Build your knowledge, immerse yourself in the latest research, attend conferences, and build your reputation as an expert in your field. Become the go-to person on that topic in your network.

Stay visible. Keep networking and growing your connections. The more you put yourself out there, the more opportunity you have to build influence.

Always Find New Opportunities to Learn

"Leadership and learning are indispensable to each other."—John F. Kennedy

It's often said that knowledge is power, but it's also said that you can't know what you don't know. From these two sayings, the need for ongoing learning becomes clear. In terms of developing your personal and professional knowledge, however, it's important to set some parameters to provide focus in your learning. To get started, consider your answers to the following questions:

What are you interested in? The interest provides motivation.

Where do you want your new knowledge to take you?

What will you need to learn to bridge the gap between where you are now and where you want to be?

Finding new opportunities to learn becomes much easier once you've established what you want to gain from furthering your skills and knowledge.

Benefits of Learning

Successful women adopt a learning mindset, meaning they are always open to and actively looking for new opportunities to learn. They view intelligence, whether academic or skills-based, as endless, and they know that there is always something new to learn—no one knows everything. If nothing else, ongoing learning is essential to keeping up with the latest advances in technology in today's fast-paced world. Studies have shown, however, that learning brings with it the added benefits of boosting confidence and building resilience. The experience of challenging oneself to learn something new creates confidence, and ongoing learning develops greater resilience not only through completing the task but also through solving problems along the way.

Learning Opportunities

As adults, learning is all too often considered too time-consuming or no longer relevant to the real world. This is because learning is associated with schools and classrooms, but learning can take many other forms.

Reading. Knowledge is power. The more you know about the field you work in or aspire to work in, the greater your potential to become a leading expert in your field. At any level in the workplace, reading industry-related books, magazines, or websites keeps you on the cutting edge, increasing your networking value and building your reputation.

Listening. The more time you spend listening to people who have greater knowledge or experienced than you, the greater your opportunity to learn from them.

Knowing what you don't know. It's only by accepting that you don't know everything that you can remain open to learning new things. Having the confidence to admit to gaps in your knowledge or understanding allows you to look for appropriate resources or experts to help you learn.

Acting. Reading and listening aren't enough. Success in any field depends on being able to put what you've learned into practice.

Teaching. Passing on your knowledge is a proven way of reinforcing your own learning.

Seeking a mentor. When you learn through a mentor, you learn through the experience of someone else. There have been many high-profile mentor-mentee relationships, but mentors can be found in all areas of life, not just in your chosen field.

Learning through Experience

During her years as CEO at Yahoo!, Marissa Mayer continued to develop her leadership skills not only through building relationships with mentors but also through keeping lines of communication open across every department and at every level in the company. She wanted to learn from the ideas and experiences of employees and then share those ideas in the boardroom. While her leadership style and overall performance at Yahoo! has been the subject of much debate, her openness to learning from every source is an essential attitude in terms of growing as a leader. "One of the best pieces of advice I've ever gotten is there are always a lot of good choices, and then there's the one you pick, commit to, and make great," she says.

Not every decision you make is guaranteed to be a great one, but there are always lessons to be learned from every outcome. Life is learning, and learning through experience is proof positive that you're trying new things and growing as a person.

Try This

To help you identify the best areas of focus for your ongoing learning, experts suggest creating a personal SWOT analysis. On a sheet of paper, draw lines to create four columns—Strengths, Weaknesses, Opportunities, and Threats.

Strengths: In this column, list your skills, qualifications, talents, experience, personal qualities, and anything else you consider to be a strength.

Weaknesses: In this column, list any areas you believe need to be addressed or improved to help you move forward in your career.

Opportunities: In this column, list potential sources of new learning that could help you to build your strengths, including formal training, informal networking, possible mentors, knowledge sharing, independent study, and so on.

Threats: In this column, list any factors or potential barriers in your environment that could get in the way of progress, limit your learning, or hold you back in any way.

Armed with this analysis, you now have the information you need to help you find new opportunities to learn and to make the most of the opportunities that are all around you every day. Knowledge is power, and power women are lifelong learners.

Lead with Power

"The most effective way to do it is to do it." —Amelia Earhart

An effective leader leads through the ability to influence others, and power adds to influence. The overall success of a leader ultimately depends on their ability to get things done, but it's their leadership style, and the power base they operate from that determines how well-liked, respected, or admired they are as a leader.

Getting Things Done ... or Just Being Bossy?

Power adds to influence, but according to the experiences of Sheryl Sandberg and other power women, successful men in leadership roles are much more likely to earn respect than women in high-ranking positions are. Confident, decisive, and in-control men are described as assertive, Sandberg says, "but women displaying the same traits are labeled bossy, aggressive, or bitchy." Assertiveness is viewed positively in men yet negatively in women, and Sandberg believes that women are being punished for exhibiting leadership traits: "Ambitious, hard-charging women violate unwritten rules about what's acceptable social conduct—and this is holding women back." Those unwritten rules revolve around outdated traditional gender stereotypes. Women are encouraged to be polite, accommodating, and nurturing, and their role should revolve around cooking, cleaning the home, and taking care of the children.

> "If more women are in leadership roles, we'll stop assuming they shouldn't be." —Sheryl Sandberg

YouTube CEO Susan Wojcicki knows a thing or two about making things happen. She's an innovative leader who continues to push Google and YouTube in new directions, placing her at No. 6 on Forbes's 2018 World's 100 Most Powerful Women list, and she's the mother of five children. She is a successful woman, but she agrees with Sandberg, commenting that despite her achievements, she's had her abilities and her commitment to her job questioned, and has been overlooked. She was excluded from industry events and social gatherings, ignored by outside leaders in meetings who chose to address her more junior (male) colleagues instead, and frequently interrupted or spoken over in the boardroom. Both Sandberg and Wojcicki have had to overcome these unwritten rules by using their attitude of success to change the attitudes of others around them.

Leading with Power

Powerful women learn how to command a room using positive body language, they learn to push themselves as they continue to push boundaries by stepping out of their comfort zone, and they learn to silence self-doubt by maintaining a growth mindset. The experiences of Sheryl Sandberg and Susan Wojcicki highlight the difficulties facing women in executive roles, but the attitudes they have adopted, it becomes clear that successful women share several traits that equip them to lead with power.

Women Who Lead with Power Are …
Passionate about what they do. It's often said that successful people do what they love and love what they do. Melinda Gates was one of the first women to hold a technical role at Microsoft, Marissa Mayer was Google's first female engineer, and Amelia Earhart was the first woman pilot to fly solo across the Atlantic. These women didn't set out be influential firsts—they were simply pursuing their passions. They chose to study and work hard to become the best they could be in the field that inspired them, and they owned their success.

Willing to step out of their comfort zone. When asked for the secret to her success, Melinda Gates said, "Get comfortable being uncomfortable." Successful women know that having the courage to keep pushing themselves is the only way to achieve their true potential. Marissa Mayer puts it this way: "I always did something I was a little not ready to do. I think that's how you grow."

Not afraid to speak up, even when their opinion is unpopular. Not everything a leader has to say will be popular, but women who lead with power are not afraid to speak their mind, initiate tough conversations, or hold their own in a debate. Maggie Kuhn, an activist, and founder of the Gray Panthers movement, once said, "Speak the truth, even if your voice shakes."

Comfortable with standing out. As Melinda Gates once said, "The world doesn't need more people who think and act the same—so resist the temptation to conform to what's around you." Women who lead with power recognize their strengths and the differences they have that make them stand out, and they choose to own and promote those abilities rather than modestly trying to blend in.

Try This

The most successful leaders inspire others to follow their lead. These seven tips from experienced leaders will help you to develop your ability to lead with power.

Lead by example. Set the tone, and others will follow your example. Be punctual, dress appropriately, be courteous, and lead through showing rather than telling.

Be a skilled communicator. Communication is a two-way street. Effective leaders make sure they are heard and understood, but they also listen to others.

Set limits. Set clear boundaries in place and stick by them. Making clear what you will and will not tolerate. Make sure you leave no room for confusion.

Demonstrate humility. Leading with power is not about making yourself the center of attention. A great leader gives credit where it's due.

Trust your team. A successful leader trusts her team to do what they do best; they avoid micromanaging.

Use head and heart. Use your head to make the best decisions for the company, but use your heart to develop healthy workplace relationships. Successful leaders are emotionally intelligent and sensitive to the needs of others.

Always keep improving. A great leader never stops learning. Seek mentors, learn from the experiences of others, and embrace every opportunity to learn new things.

Women are choosing to go to work. They want to work.

Women want to return to work.

Perhaps they recently had a baby, have been home for a few years with children, or their children have moved on to college or university and maybe starting a family of their own. Whatever the reason, women want to enter or re-enter the workforce after having taken a period out for family reasons.

Tips for women already in the workplace who want to further their career.

When a woman is considering leaving a job for maternity reasons, how long she is on leave for and when she returns could be directly influenced by a company or country's leave policy. Depending on her circumstances, these policies about her financial and professional position could play a major role – primarily if it offers paid or unpaid leave, which are due to eligibility requirements, and flexibility.

Country Options

Australia

Australia offers a plan for women leaving work for maternity reasons that provides up to 52 weeks of leave, though it is all unpaid. In January 2011 the Australian government introduced a paid parental leave scheme (you will need to review the website to see if you are eligible for the scheme). Still, studies have shown that the average point at which women return to work is 18 months after giving birth. At this point, it is estimated that about 54% of women return to work with only about 43% of these being permanent employees. Another 7% move into becoming self-employed. What is also interesting about this number is that of the women who returned after 18 months, 84% had been working before they left for maternity leave compared to just 13% who had not previously held jobs.

For mothers in Australia, the number of children they have tends to be another factor in deciding whether to return to work. It was found that women with three children or more are 10% less likely to work outside the home than women with two or fewer children. An estimated 68% of women who had two or fewer children were employed outside the home compared to just 55% of women with three or more children.

In a 2010 follow-up study to the 2005 data from the Center for Work-life policy (CWLP), it was found that, on average, women return to work just over two and a half years after giving birth. One reason for the delay, according to the CWLP study, was that nearly two-thirds of the women were having a difficult time finding a job. Also, 16% said they took a significant pay cut when they did find a job.

United States

A three-year survey conducted by the United States Census Bureau on women returning to work found that, on average, women who had children returned after about a year of having the child. The survey supported the fact that when women stay at home with the children instead of working, the household has a lower income. In fact, it was found that 45% of the mothers who stayed at home made less than $50,000 a year compared with about 25% of the working mothers who fell in the same bracket. Similarly, fewer work-at-home mothers made over $100,000 compared to mothers who worked outside the home.

Interestingly, the survey showed that 64% of mothers with children over the age of two years were already back in the workforce. However, what made the study even more interesting was that it pointed out how women who had been working outside the home before having a child, we're hesitant to leave the job at all. They were even hesitant to become pregnant, because of the personal, as well as the professional, image they had accrued and all the time and investment they had made in creating and cultivating that image.

In the United States, the Family Leave Act (FMLA) was enacted in 1993 to provide job protection for up to 12 weeks within 12 months. The program is intended to cover any medical-type situation, from health issues to taking care of parents and more. So for qualifying mothers, FMLA would be the program which would cover maternity in most situations. There are a few companies that may offer employees a maternity plan, though it would be subject to the company's own independent criteria.

With regards to FMLA, about 25% of employers offer fully paid leave for the duration of the period the employee is on FMLA, with 20% offering no pay at all about maternity leave. FMLA has additional limitations. For example, FMLA does not apply to small businesses, generally because they can't afford to be without employees, even for a few months. This leaves nearly 40% of United States workers without this program as an option.

The United States is considered to be relatively low on the scale of countries that offer strong policies to women who leave a job due to maternity, and more so, who want to return to work. Even with the FMLA, which is supposed to guarantee positions are held for employees who qualify, often it is not enough.

Another issue with the FMLA program is that while it is government mandated and supported, each state is responsible for handling the FMLA program. Further, there are many exceptions to the policy which leads the program to be handed down to the company as their responsibility. This results in an inconsistent and unbalanced system related to this plan.

The numbers related to women working in the United States since 2007 have become disturbing. A recent news report noted that women were way behind in getting the available jobs with men stepping into almost 90% of them. The report justified the unbalanced numbers by saying that men had lost relatively more jobs than women since 2007 when the recession began – almost 2:1.

Speaking in more recent terms, the numbers in the first quarter of 2012 in the United States showed that men lost an estimated 16,000 jobs while women lost nearly 484,000. Meanwhile, in gains over the last 12 months, men entered 1.9 million jobs while women entered 635,000; accounting for about 25% of the available positions. However, numbers have been as low as 10% related to women taking available jobs.

Nearly all of the articles and sources reporting the job situation reflect that men have been able to recover better than women have during this recessionary period. One of the causes why women have lost more jobs, is because of their general work sector. Women tend to be more concentrated in job positions, including government, manufacturing, retail, and teaching jobs, which are areas that have seen considerable layoffs over the last few years. Meanwhile, men have been more flexible over the board with job types.

While women lost more jobs, men gained more in local government and utility positions. The primary sectors where men lost positions were in construction and manufacturing. However, women did seem to excel in services and health services jobs. Also, women have been less likely to be moved up into management positions, with only 31% being promoted compared to 36% of their male counterparts.

Women-owned businesses in the United States employ nearly 38% of the workers in the country, according to the National Association of Women Business Owners. Therefore, in the over 9 million women-owned businesses, they are employing over 27 million people! Another interesting number in the United States is that women are the main breadwinners in nearly a third of the households.

Also, based on information from the United States Department of Labor, there has been a noticeable increase in women who choose to work-at-home. It is estimated that over 5.6 million women are stay-at-home moms. These positions come from a variety of locations, from self-starting businesses to work-at-home (WAH) jobs from companies that are looking to cut expenses and overhead.

United Kingdom

The United Kingdom's policy on maternity leave offers women 12 weeks of paid leave time and up to an additional 53 weeks of unpaid time. The pay during the first 12 weeks is about 90% of the employee's pay during the first six weeks then a flat rate for the last six. The employer, however, is refunded 92%, which comes from public funds. The United Kingdom offers new mothers what are called "keep in touch" days where women can work up to a total of ten days during their maternity leave.

The greatest issue facing women in the United Kingdom today is from the concern that if she stays away from the workplace for prolonged periods, whether she had a career before taking time off or is new to the workforce, that she may not be able to find work. This is a valid concern. It is estimated that it could take a woman, on average, two years to find a job. Add to that the fact that childcare is on the rise, increasing about 6% in 2011.

Recent numbers for the United Kingdom shows that 2.67 million people are unemployed with 1.12 million being women. Also, it appeared that women were losing their jobs at a faster rate than men. As an example, in Scotland, where one-third of the jobs in the United Kingdom are being lost, on average, 400 women per day are losing their jobs.

One of the areas where women hold a substantial number of positions is in the public sector, which looks to be hit hard these last few years, especially retail. And of the new jobs being created, only one of six positions have been filled by women. Meanwhile, the ratio of full-time workers is nearly 2:1 man over women, respectively.

Canada

Women in Canada can take 15 weeks of paid leave and then up to another 35 weeks with 55% pay of their weekly earnings. Canada allows women to work on a part-time basis up to a certain earning amount, though this varies by province.

One of the main issues facing women in Canada is the stress of going to work too soon. This appears to cause anxiety and results in lost days of work and possible termination from the job. Yet the issue appears to depend on the income level of the mother. For instance, women making greater salaries have increased income and better overall attitude on the job and with the family, as well as being able to provide better childcare.

Similar issues have abounded in Canada with fields where women dominate hit hard. For instance, when Canada downsized its postal service, 3,000 people were let go with 83% being women. To add to the stresses of not finding jobs and women being let go from the workforce, it adds to the problem when the men in the household lose their jobs as well. Women are then called upon not only to try and find a job but to emotionally support the men who are also looking. Thus women have shown an increase in depression symptoms over the last few years.

New Zealand

In New Zealand, parents are allowed 14 weeks of paid leave and up to 38 weeks of unpaid time. Interestingly, the majority of women in New Zealand tend to hold part-time jobs rather than full-time. It's estimated that this is the case for over 70% of the women working in New Zealand. The primary field for women is in the service industries.

How to succeed with a job they already have and want to advance and get a promotion

The world is suffering, not just about jobs but in regards to trades. The problem truly is worldwide. Examples of trade jobs are electricians, plumbers, warehouse workers, welders, and mechanics. The problem is that the new generations aren't interested in these positions. Once the older generations retire, there will be few replacements. However, the problem is deeper than this. The global economy has shut down much of the work in these fields. There is less new construction in residential or commercial areas. Trades require apprenticeships or training hours as well as schooling. Therefore, according to several union representatives, by the time the economy improves and building increases, there won't be people coming out of the apprentice programs to fill the need. What's more, no one wants them. It's been suggested time and again over the years that these positions could be very successfully filled by women.

In Canada, for instance, over one million skilled jobs need to be filled. They need engineers and computer tech people. Australia has indicated that they have the same shortages. In the United States, most apprenticeships are supported by unions which are under fire from the government for such reasons as adhering to higher safety codes and maintaining wages. Both of these are more costly to the prospective employer than if they used "unskilled" laborers.

In Europe, in general, it is shown that women made up half of the numbers to men in the field of agriculture, one quarter in industrial jobs, and about the same numbers in service jobs. However, women showed higher unemployment rates than men did, 12% to 7% respectively.

While women are tipping off dominance in many fields worldwide, in the United States, women have succeeded in passing men in the fields of accounting, financial managers, resource managers, meeting planners, registered nurses, veterinarians, and psychology in the past ten years.

A short discussion on returning to work after divorce

Sources cite that in the case of divorce, the average income for the family typically drops by 37%. Granted, there may be child support and alimony, but it's not usually nearly enough to compensate for the financial loss. There will be expenses that likely won't be covered. Therefore, this forces most women to consider going to work.

Divorce is fairly common. In the United States, it's estimated that 49% of marriages will end in divorce. In Canada, it's 45%, Australia 46%, United Kingdom 43%, and in New Zealand, it's about 46%. One disturbing statistic about women and divorce is that of the women who return to work, 40% of the families with women working as a head of household are under the poverty line in the United States. A study in the United Kingdom showed that after divorce, men's incomes tended to increase by 11% while women lost 17%.

Why Women Return to Work

For many women, the idea of working is as much a social, psychological, and mental need as it is for their male counterparts. Most societies encourage men working outside the home and seemingly always have. However, that wasn't usually the case for women.

Benefits of working outside the home

For women, holding a job outside the home has several benefits. It offers the opportunity to be well rounded as people, as role models and as empowered members of society. It's interesting to consider the relationship between what is accepted today and what things were like not even fifty years ago. In most countries, the view of women working outside the home has dramatically shifted.

History

If we take an interesting trek into the not-really-too-distant past, we may see the amazing journey that women have taken to reach the place they are today. Today, most women have held a job outside of the home during some point in their lives. Modern generations actually take for granted the assumption they will have a job or a career, yet it wasn't always that way.

In most countries, a hundred years ago, women were homemakers. The women who typically worked outside the home were impoverished or in the minority. The only jobs they held tended to be traditional female roles such as seamstresses and weavers in shops or factories. They may have worked as domestic help, store clerks, nannies, cooks, nurses, and midwives typists, secretaries, stenographers, and telephone operators. Some countries did allow women to be teachers, though many had the added stipulation that the woman would not be married.

One popular career choice for several women was writing. However, most successful authors of the day had to write under male pseudonyms. To be fair, a few women did bend the norm from time to time by becoming doctors or lawyers, though these cases were quite rare.

For many countries, the benchmark of changes for women working outside the home in greater numbers and in a wider variety of occupations came with two events. One was the point where countries gave women the same rights to vote as men. However, the second seemed to be the most common for larger nations and had appeared to have changed the way that societies saw women in the workplace forever: World War II.

In Australia, during World War II, the country asked women to fill the jobs vacated by men who went off to war. These included jobs in factories, transportation, commerce, and even public service. Although women only earned up to 75% of what the men had earned at the same job. The male-dominated unions actually strongly opposed women being in the jobs and were instrumental in removing women from those roles once the war ended. However, women proved to the country that they were more than capable (and in some cases, better) of doing the jobs. Thus, societal views on women's abilities to work outside the home had forever been changed.

In the United States, the image of "Rosie the Riveter" symbolized the women's movement into jobs that were, at the time, not traditional to them. However, because of the war, women were thrust into these jobs.

The patriotic slogan for the Rosie posters was "We Can Do It." There were several slogans the government had used to recruit women such as, "The more women at work, the sooner we win" and "Women, you could hasten victory by working and save your man." But really, it didn't take a lot of prodding to get women to voluntarily move from their lower-waged jobs – from behind vacuum cleaners and even out of school – to answer the call to work in the factories and non-traditional jobs the government was recruiting for.

There were over 6 million women who stepped up in 1942 (over 18 million by 1944) and did everything from operating machinery to delivering mail. More than that, the barriers were broken. Women of all economic statuses and minorities worked side by side earning good wages (though still only at 60% of what the men had made doing the same job) and demonstrating to the nation that women were more than capable of handling any job.

Rosie was actually an illustration by Norman Rockwell for the cover of an edition of the Saturday Evening Post in 1943. The model had been Rose Will Monroe, a factory worker at the Ford Motor Company's aircraft assembly plant. A second Rosie inspiration was Rose Hicker, who worked at an airplane manufacturing plant.

The term "Rosie the Riveter" actually came out in a song in 1942 by Redd Evans and John Jacob Loeb. In the song was a famous lyric that went "that frail little girl can do more than a man can do."

As the war ended and men returned home, once again as it was in most countries, millions of women were fired and forced to return to low-paying jobs or back to their domestic positions. However, the seed had been planted, and many women forged forward to continue the process of change to allow women back into the higher-paying workforce.

Canada had a similar history where the war was the catalyst for women entering the workforce outside the home, though in this case, it began in World War I. At that time, the country needed laborers and called out primarily to unmarried women to fill them while the men went to war. Women mostly held jobs such as typists, secretaries, and factory workers with nearly 35,000 being employed by 1917, the same year that Canada gave women the right to vote.

The depression of 1930 forced women back into their previous domestic duties until about 1942 when another labor shortage forced the country to call out again to women. This time, however, it wasn't just the unmarried women who were asked to fill positions outside the home but also married women and women with children. By 1945, it was estimated that one-third of the women in Canada were employed outside the home.

Similar to the United States, Canadian women took jobs in almost every field during World War II. They worked as scientists, in ammunition and explosive factories, service jobs and almost every other job that men had previously occupied.

Canada had its own version of "Rosie the Riveter" – "Ronnie, the Bren Gun Girl." Ronnie, who was modeled after Veronica Foster, represented over one million Canadian women who had answered the country's call to work in the factories during the war. And, like the women in the United States and elsewhere, when the war was over, the Canadian women were told in essence to go home, but they did not want to return to domestic life.

Britain saw an interesting situation happen. During World War I, the country had enough women step up and volunteer to take positions needed to keep the country running in the absence of the men at war that they didn't feel they needed to do much else. But in World War II, it wasn't enough. They needed more hands. In 1940, a secret report explained that there was a need to hire women to fill the voids. In 1941, Britain required women aged 18-60 to register, be interviewed, and take a job from the range which was offered to the individual. This led to the National Service Act in 1941, which legalized women to be able to work. By 1943, it was estimated that as many as 90% of single women and 80% of married women were working outside the home. And, yes, like everywhere else, when the war ended, women were sent home.

In Britain, too, World War I and II saw the formulation and the call for women to join the Women's Land Army, also called Land Girls.

When men left for war, women were asked to tend to the fields to produce the food. The United States and Australia had similar groups during the same time, modeling Britain's program.

Britain established the Women's Timber Corps during World War II, with the women who joined being known as "Lumber Jills." The Lumber Jills handled many aspects of forestry, including operating sawmills, driving trucks, loading, and crosscutting.

In Britain, women were given the rights to vote in 1928. Many believed it was because of World War I. And, as with most countries, women entered the workforce in droves during World War II – an estimated 40%. And, like with other countries, women didn't want to give up their jobs. In some cases, single and widowed women fought for the right to work over married women, and in some jobs, married women were actually banned for some time.

The Australian Women's Land Army offered another valuable benefit to the country – equality. On the farms, women from all educational and other types of backgrounds lived and worked side by side and were considered equal.

Women in Australia were given the right to vote in 1901 and 1902, and it did take over 40 years for women to make their significant dent in the image of women in the workforce. Interestingly enough, though, in New Zealand, women were allowed to vote as early as 1893, yet the country had strongly encouraged women to hold their domestic status.

Why are women going back to work today?

There are a variety of reasons why women desire to return to the workforce. One is, of course, due to the financial need for the family. For example, women who have just given birth and are single mothers trying to make it on one income tend to need to return to work as soon as possible. On the other hand, women who are in two-income households want to return to work for several possible reasons. Five of the most commonly noted reasons why women work include:

   * Money; earn, contribute

   * Feeling she can make it on her own if she needed (or wanted) to; pull own weight in the household, justify own spending, independence, and validation

   * For a sense of accomplishment, intellectual stimulation, personal growth, validation

   * Social interaction outside the home, associate with like-minded people

   * Inspire others; show children that they can be anything they want to be.

Studies have found that women who work are less depressed than women who don't. A recent study by the American Psychological Association (Buehler, Cheryl and Marion O'Brien, Mothers' Part-Time Employment: Associations With Mother and Family Well-Being, American Psychological Association, 2011, Vol 25, No. 6, P895-906) showed that women who work, even part-time, were happier and healthier than women who don't work at all. Besides mental and physical health, the study mentioned that women tended to be more attentive, sensitive, and patient with younger children and participated more with their school-aged children's events than did unemployed mothers.

For some women, they had careers before they had children, and after having them, wanted to return to their careers. Some women like the freedom of having job offers. And with more opportunities available to women than ever before, women have many places to grow. Besides that, most women simply like to work.

Money is the primary motivation

Several sources cite that money is, and always has been, the primary motivator for women going to or returning to work. One challenge women may find in returning to work is the changes in the economic climate. Basically, this simply requires a more creative expression of a person's skills and a more aggressive effort in seeking employment. For women who can return to an old employer or who have contacts in other companies, these are great benefits. More will be discussed throughout this book on how to best handle the situation and present the skills to get those jobs.

How do you begin the Switching industries?

The time has come. You made a choice, for whatever reason, to return to the workforce. So what now? What is the next step? How do you begin the process of finding work?

The best strategy for getting back to work is to have a well laid out plan. This will help you in many ways. A well laid out plan is like a map that can take you from where you are to where you want to go. Many call this a goal.

When you use a map or a goal, you will have a path to follow to reach your ultimate destination of finding a job. When you are looking at a map, don't you usually break the trek down into parts? For instance, you might find you need to travel on this road for a while then turn onto another, pass through a town where you might have to meander through a few town streets to reach the next highway, and so forth. Every time you make that change, catch that new road, you are that much closer to your end result.

Have you ever mapped out a trip? Maybe it was across town or over a long distance. Yet you may have cheered as you made another turn or caught another road, excited that, wow, you made it halfway, or whatever the case may have been. These are celebrations. They make you feel good that you are getting closer to that destination! Therefore, when you have been on your path of looking for a job for a while and made a turn onto the next path, celebrate! It's exciting! And it helps keep your spirits up to continue through the process.

Making a goal

Most people have heard about goals. Basically, it's a plan that you make for yourself that has a final destination, in this case having a job. When you set a goal, you need some important ingredients:

* You need a specific result to work towards. Narrow down what, how, and why.

* It needs to be broken down into actual and workable timeframes – actual dates – specific when.

* Make it achievable. If you want to be a doctor in a month and have never taken a medical class, it's not likely you will achieve your goal. It must be something that you can do. It's okay if it is a bit of a challenge, just not completely out of the ballpark. Push yourself a little bit beyond what you already know

The most important point to keep in mind about making a goal around finding a job is to keep your end result realistic. Can you achieve your goal? Can you do what it takes to accomplish it? Are your timeframes realistic? Ask these questions for each step of the process. Is it realistic? If so, great. If not, make the necessary adjustments. You don't want to stop yourself cold before you ever give yourself a chance to succeed.

Additional brainstorming

Now we are moving on to making several lists. By putting in the time to make these lists, you can save a lot of time down the road. The information here can be used through the whole process of reaching that end result.

Begin with a list about your job experience or interests

If you have worked or done volunteer work in the past, note all of your experiences on the job. What you did? What you learned? What certifications did you get? And so on. There are even job skills that can be gained from working at home. For instance, if you enjoyed landscaping, dealing with plants and flowers, and learned a lot about them, you may want to use that knowledge to become a landscaper or florist. For people who are new to working and aren't sure about what you want to do, you can still make a list of your interests or jobs and then do some research to see what kinds of jobs related to those interests.

From this list, make sub-lists. You can note things like:

* Associations and clubs you might be able to join to get contacts and stay updated on recent trends or changes in your job field. This is a great networking opportunity.

* Enquire to see if you need to update certificates to meet current demands.

* Anything else that comes to mind related to this topic.

The steps to the goal

As you look over what you have done already in this chapter, you should see that you have a lot of great information. Now we will take this and move forward to creating two more pieces of the puzzle. These two will actually be your action parts – the pieces that you will work from to achieve your goal. One is the large action plan itself, and the other is a daily plan.

The action plan

Here is where we will bring together your goal statement and your lists to create an action plan. The plan starts where you are right now and ends with the first line of your goal statement of what you want to do. Therefore, if you were to draw a line across the paper, the first point would be now, today, and the end of the line would be your goal with that date attached to it.

If you look at the rest of the line, those are all the stepping stones to get from today to the goal. We will need to fill in those stepping stones based on the information in your statement and lists.

You may already have some ideas on how to reach that goal. If so, write them down. If you don't know how to get to your goal from where you are right now, that's okay, too. We will go through an example that will help you to fill in those points.

Something to be sure of and consider is to make your stepping stones workable and achievable. Break them down into do-able pieces. It may seem to people who have been in the workplace before that there can be steps removed because you already know those parts or have things in play, so you don't need to necessarily do them again.

Here is the thing. Keeping a clear, process-oriented path of your progress is useful for complete the goal. So if one of your stepping stones is to join a group to network and you have already done that, great. However, put it in your steps anyway. You can say you have done it but more than that, it is a reminder to actually use that group, go to meetings, network, and follow up which are very important pieces to getting where you want to be. So don't delete steps.

Another important point to keep in mind is making steps do-able. This means keeping them small and making sure they are things you can accomplish. For instance, if you have a goal to get a job in 12 months, and one of your stepping stones says, "get a two-year certification," you are keeping yourself from achieving your goal.

Some stepping stones can become goals in themselves. For instance, in getting a two-year certification, if it doesn't keep you from getting into a job, that can be a goal with its own stepping stones. If it keeps you from getting a job now, either extend your goal date further out (at some point after you get the certification) or, as we will see in a few moments, expand your options to accept a slightly different job until you can get your certificate and go into the one you do truly want.

You will no doubt find plenty of factors that will play havoc with your timeline. Things might change as you move along, and you need to be flexible when necessary. For the most part, though, the stepping stones should be pretty much set. To demonstrate this, let's look at a partial example.

First, let's take your goal statement into consideration. Remember, you want to keep it specific and motivating. This means that your goal statement should not say something like: "I want to get a job sometime. I'm not sure when or if I can, but it's what I want." Besides being very general, this statement isn't very motivating.

A better statement may be: "I want to return to work in a Fortune 500 company in a position of middle management where I am overseeing 20-50 people based on my experience in past years. I have exemplary supervisory skills earned from three past job positions. I am a great leader and teacher and have excellent interpersonal skills. I will truly make a difference with my team. I will be in a middle management position by March 31, 2013."

You can see how, in this second statement, there are specific details and uplifting, motivating statements. There is a lot of information that we can use. We see from this statement that this person wants:

* A middle management job, overseeing 20-50 people.

* To work in a Fortune 500 company (this can narrow down the research to Fortune 500 companies).

With all of the information in this statement, you can see how it will be useful in keeping this person on track toward reaching their goal. Next, we want to make some stepping stones.

In our example, this person has a lot of experience and is very specific. In reality, the stepping stones may depend on several personal factors, including where along the process they are today. If we assume this is just at the beginning point of looking for work, and you have been out of the marketplace for a couple of years, you have two small children at home, you take care of the house and meals as well as errands, then you will need to structure the "workday" to fill this as well.

One thing that will happen as the "workday" is integrated into the regular day is you will need to have better time management. You will find ways to prioritize tasks to find the time to do these steps and thereby to achieve the goal. The timeline may be affected more significantly at first as the routines will change, and a new routine will need to be created. Because of this, the timeline estimates may be a little off, and you might have to make changes to them.

To illustrate this, we'll create a few possible stepping stones for the path. We'll start with where you are today and remind ourselves where you want to be at the end:

* Today: Just starting out on the path of reaching my goal – date, March 31, 2012.

* Goal: To have a job where I am managing 20-50 people in a Fortune 500 company by March 31, 2013.

Now, let's fill in some of the stones:

* Today: Just starting out on the path of reaching my goal – date, March 31, 2012

[Task and date]

* Research the market for Fortune 500 companies. Have a list of companies by April 15, 2012

* Create a resume and a cover letter template to submit as opportunities arise. Gather details of old positions related to this job including companies, duties, certifications, etc. and have done by May 1, 2012

* Research, the companies from the list. Are there expansions going on, mergers, opportunities appearing to open up in the future? Have research done by May 15, 2012.

* Look at job boards, websites and find other places to search for management jobs. Have a list in place by May 15, 2012; check boards ongoing.

* Make a list of resources I could use such as people I worked with, people I know in the industry, groups and have the list ready by June 1, 2012.

* Contact resources weekly, one to two and follow-up as necessary; ongoing.

We'll pause here, but in your actual plan, you want to go all the way to the end.

In this example, however, do you see how specific and do-able the stones are? Some will be able to be done quickly, while some will take some time, and others will continue to be worked on over the duration. As each stone is met, for instance, doing the research, making the contacts, and doing the resume, you can see how with each step, you get closer to your goal!

Daily plan

Similarly to how the action plan takes you from today to your goal using stepping stones, the daily plan takes you through the course of the day to meet those steps. It's a way to block out times of the day, deal with the steps set for that day, and help to keep track of measurable results.

Part of the goal of the day planner is to begin to see times during your day where you can fit in these "work" activities. Then as you begin to manage time better by, say, prioritizing tasks, you will begin to see that you will have more time to devote to your stepping stones.

More on goals

You may need to make other changes to your life as well. These need to be incorporated in achieving your main goal of getting a job because they may have a direct impact on or directly be impacted by your decision to return to work.

Let's talk a moment about two more aspects of goals: why they don't work and how to help make them work.

Why goals don't work

There are several reasons why goals aren't met. Keeping a focus on the end result while working on it in workable pieces is priceless and gives you the best chance of succeeding. Another important factor is staying motivated.

This is why it is imperative to keep your goals realistic and the stepping stones reachable. When people create goals which they can't reach, the whole process tends to end quickly and in a fury of frustration. So make your goal realistic and something you can accomplish.

As we just mentioned, it is crucial to break the steps into workable pieces. It's much easier to take six small steps rather than six giant steps. Because finishing each step is a measuring stick toward reaching the ultimate goal, you want to be able to see the progress. As you do complete steps, remember to congratulate yourself. You did, after all, succeed in that step and staying upbeat and excited will help to maintain that momentum you need to keep going.

Sometimes you won't take a step. Sometimes things happen, and the direction might need to change, or the timeline might have to be adjusted. It's okay to change direction if you need to accomplish what you want to do. Be sure to give yourself that permission.

At times, setting actual dates for stepping stones can be tricky. It is important to set dates because when people leave tasks open to be completed whenever there isn't as much motivation to actually complete it. As you look at your daily schedule as it is, you might be thinking that setting dates is basically setting yourself up for failure.

There are always things that are out of your control. Yet the purpose of setting dates is to help you stay motivated, to help you keep you on track and on task, and to help you to see progress. Sure it might change, though the more you can keep to the schedule, the sooner you will see your desired outcome.

How to help succeed with your goals

The best way to help succeed in reaching your goal is simply to stay and keep doing it. Even if you falter, get back up and move forward.

We have talked about some other ways to succeed, and we will touch on them again here:

Make and keep steps of the goals realistic and do-able

Make the timeframes achievable

Keep an eye on the big picture. As we know us, women are always looking at the big picture, so make sure you look at the big picture for your self. The issue is getting there by taking the steps. Stay on the path but keep the end in mind as motivation. Check-in now and then to be sure that you are still moving in the right direction and following your steps. Check that your objective is still clear.

Get yourself in the right frame of mind right from the start

At the start of each day, as you prepare to go to "work," picture yourself succeeding at the day's tasks. Read your goal statement. Do anything else that gets you revved up in the morning!

Celebrate the small things!

If you are only waiting for the end result to happen to celebrate, you are selling yourself short of all of the opportunities and achievements you have succeeded. You may not want to celebrate everything, and that's fine. But you should find opportunities to be excited and pat yourself on the back when you complete tasks.

Surround yourself with support

Remember that list you made of people who you feel would support your goals? Use it.

Like we mentioned, sometimes things happen that are out of your control or as you start to work on the steps, you find the dates for some pieces aren't realistic. It's okay to modify things if you need to. Obviously, you don't want to change your entire plan because that takes the wind out of your sails. You will lose momentum, excitement, and motivation if you constantly have to make changes. This is why it is useful to make the lists, do the research, and whatever else you need to have at the onset to make the process workable. Still, sometimes, there do need to be changes made. Make them, and continue forward toward your goal!

Checklist

This chapter has covered a lot of information on setting goals, making lists, creating stepping stones to reach the goal, and being open to options and making changes. We have discussed some additional considerations you may want to keep in mind when making the decision to go back to work. To close out this chapter, here is a convenient checklist for you to help keep you on track to get what you want!

Goals

* Do the research.

* Set a specific date to meet your goal by.

* The date is achievable.

* The goal and date are realistic.

* You created a short goal statement.

* You wrote out a list of job experience skills and interests.

* You made a sub-list of resources you can use to help achieve the goal, such as networking opportunities and clubs.

* A list of mentors.

* You made a list of things you like to do to have balance in your life.

* You made an action plan with stepping stones in writing.

* You have a daily planner in place.

* You have an optional weekly planner in place.

* You have deliverables in the plan so you can measure progress.

* If applicable: Researched school degree or certification programs.

* If applicable: Enrolled in school.

* Fell off of the path toward your goal but returned and continued forward.

* Celebrate successes.

* Use the mentor list.

Considerations and compromises

* Have stress-reducing tools in place.

The Corporate World

Women from all levels of the corporate ladder have left their positions at one time or another and made the transition back into various corporate roles. Probably the most well-told example is Brenda Barnes, who left her Chief Executive Officer (CEO) position at PepsiCo, where she was earning $2 million a year, to stay at home with her three children. After seven years, Barnes returned to the corporate world, joining Sara Lee as the Chief Operating Officer (COO) and a year later, becoming their CEO.

Barnes expressed in one of her interviews that it was important for women who wanted to return to corporate work to keep up on what was going on in the corporate world. In addition, Barnes set a useful and real-life example where, when she decided to re-enter the corporate arena, she had done so by using her experience to get back into the corporate environment even though it hadn't been initially at her prior position of CEO, and worked her way back up to where she'd wanted to be.

Some women who opted to leave the corporate world for the family may believe that they are somehow "less than" if they do not return to the workforce in the same capacity in which they'd left it. People in this frame of mind have reported concerns of not being respected, not being considered for higher positions, or not even being seen as capable (especially if the corporate landscaping has changed a lot and there are fewer familiar faces).

For Barnes, this idea held a familiar ring. She had relayed in another interview that she had to learn to back off her identity a bit – to realize that her job wasn't her entire image and description of her personal value.

For many women, part of the transition of stepping back into the working world is about making that separation from how she used to see herself at work and how she sees herself now. With a family, where a part of a woman's identity is with the children of the household, she may feel less "whole" or not as completely immersed on the job as she may have been pre-family.

For most women, working outside the home provides a sense of purpose, value, and identity. These traits will continue forward when she returns to work; however, there will be that added component of being a mother. Because of this, there will be some inner turmoil around how she may have remembered work to be pre-family and how it will be when she returns to work.

Besides this psychological aspect, there are others. For instance, some women might have to deal with entering the corporate world at a lower level on the ladder than they had been at when she'd left the job. This takes adjusting in itself, such as in earnings and responsibilities. There may be some inner turmoil around getting promotions and rekindling that ambition for doing so. This said it doesn't at all mean that a woman can't return to work and be productive, valuable, and feel good about what she is doing on the job!

Changing Careers

For women who have worked in a particular field and feel they would like to change, they should consider asking themselves: Why? – What is the reason behind wanting to look into other careers?

* Are you burned out?

* Are you frustrated?

* Do you want more flexibility in your schedule?

* Are you not seeing the opportunities you wanted or thought you would?

* Are you not seeing yourself doing the job in ten years?

* Did you happen to fall into your current job and now would like to do something you want to do?

These are important considerations because once a woman realizes the reason behind her decision to change careers, she will have some momentum behind that decision. Without momentum, likely, she won't succeed in the direction she wants to go.

What to consider when making a career change

When considering a career change, do some research. Look at sources such as job outlook tools on-line or at the library. Talk to people who are already working in the job. Read trade magazines. Consider finding a mentor. And realize that you won't be a seasoned professional at the career for a while so absorb all the information that you can early on in the process.

Find out what is involved in doing the job; what education or experience will you need, and how can you get that experience? It will help to see how much time you may need before you can begin to earn a living at the new career. If it looks like it might take a little bit of time, be sure to check that your financial situation can accommodate the timeframe without putting added stress financially on the family.

Some companies offer internal training programs, also called cross-training. With these programs, employees can learn skills in performing jobs in other areas of the company. So this provides one way of learning a new skill while also working. Also, some companies offer financial assistance for employees who want to take higher education courses and/or earn a degree.

Of course, when considering a career change, many people become concerned about age issues. For people who work in physical environments, this may be a real consideration. In many other fields, this might not be as significant. For women over the age of 40 considering career changes, sources report that jobs including nursing, working in the non-profit sector, accounting, computer sciences, education, human resources, crisis management, consulting, and working at home as some popular choices.

Working out of home

Self-employment, working for yourself and being your own boss, is growing as an option for women who want to work and have a family or just want to not fulfill someone else's dream! A large benefit to this type of work is, of course, the flexibility. As your own boss, you set your own hours.

Ideas for self-employment are unlimited. Interested in travel? – Be a travel writer. Have extensive experience in your field? – Be a consultant. Good at being an assistant? – Use your skills as a virtual assistant. Almost every idea you have can be the basis for an at-home business. Additionally, some companies now offer work-at-home (WAH) programs. These programs help with a company's overhead costs because they don't have to house employees. The employees work out of their own homes. Also, many online job sites offer virtual or work-at-home opportunities as a searchable term.

If you are interested in entering into self-employment, you aren't alone. In Australia, 30% of the over 2 million self-employed people are women. Of these, 5% work in trades. Additionally, nearly 33% of women working for themselves are professional women in the technical and sciences fields.

In New Zealand, the numbers of self-employed women are on the rise; estimated to be over 36% of the total self-employed group. However, it is noted that self-employed women tended to earn less money than women who hold regular jobs. It is estimated that of the self-employed women, about 41% work an estimated five hours per day compared to those engaged in full-time employment.

Women in the United Kingdom have shown a slight increase in the number of those being self-employed. Based on statistics from 2000 to 2007, women who have become self-employed have shown an increase of 17%; accounting for about 27% of all self-employed people. The most common fields for self-employed women included administration, finance, and other service-oriented areas.

Canada shows more women in the current generation entering self-employment than any previous generation. About 10% of those who work from home do so for other companies. Self-employed women make up about 33% of the self-employed workers in Canada. Canada is second only to the United States in purchasing franchises as a means of self-employment.

In the United States, just under 25% of working women work in the home. Of these, about 5.5% are self-employed while the remainder works for companies and/or in a virtual capacity. Per employment data, over 20% of women with children work in sales and office jobs, followed closely behind by service occupations and management positions.

A few considerations for working out of home

Working out of the home requires a few traits that working outside the home doesn't necessarily require, such as discipline, time management, organization, and saying "no" regularly. Working at home requires a lot of focus and discipline. It is easier to get distracted at home with friends, television, as well as thinking about your to-do list. Because it is so easy to get distracted, it is more important to be able to stay focused on the task to get it done.

Managing time, especially if you are only working part-time, is essential to functioning well at home. With a limited amount of time to work, the time needs to be used effectively and efficiently and on task.

So having top-notch organizational skills will help keep things in-line and on-task. Organizational skills can include things like making lists, having an efficient filing system, staying relatively clutter-free, and so forth.

And saying "no" to friends who call for lunch or just to talk, the family who calls that need something or other such distractions will keep you on track. Working out of the house is just like having a job outside the house, only you are more accessible and, as such, need to put realistic boundaries in place. These boundaries become your proverbial brick-and-mortar walls until it's quitting time.

Another consideration when thinking about what to do as a self-employed person includes taking into account the work environment. If, for instance, there is a lot of noise in the home, maybe a phone-type job won't be as optimum as say, typing, writing, or research, which generally requires much less phone time.

Checklist

* Decide what you are going to enter or re-enter the working world as in terms of career.

* Is returning to the previous company an option? If so, have you made connections with the appropriate people to let them know you are interested in coming back to work?

* Research the latest market information on that career.

* Decide what you need to do to get up to date on your career (schooling, licensure, or something else).

* Be open to entering the workforce at a different level or in a different aspect of that career from which you left it.

* Check your level of worth and value.

* If applicable, check on companies with re-entry or on-ramping type programs.

* If applicable, check with local colleges or work centers to get updated on workplace skills.

* Interested in changing careers? Ask yourself why? Is this reason motivational?

* Interested in working out of home? Check into options.

* Establish a specific time schedule and organization plan to follow to work out of the home.

Telecommuting

We've been talking about a rather vague array of work-at-home opportunities. Let's begin getting more specific by identifying one particular type of WAH employee: those who work for a company though do so from their own home.

People who work from home for a company have many titles, including telecommuters, teleworkers, virtual workers, or remote workers. Others, such as people who travel a lot rather than stay strictly at a home location or an on-site office, are often called "mobile" or "portable" professionals.

Besides the noted benefits to the employee for working at home, telecommuting opportunities allow for people to find jobs from nearly any location. This expands the job market for those looking for work. Employees report being more motivated in working from home, which leads to better customer service and fewer workplace problems, which result in lost productivity on the job site.

For the company itself, there is less overhead costs, less cost for real estate and utilities as well as maintenance and upkeep. Companies found that WAH employees tend to be more productive and have less downtime and take fewer days off. Some companies report as much as 40% improved productivity with telecommuters.

A few concerns for the company using teleworkers are a decrease in security and priority information, less personal interaction with supervisors for monitoring and coaching, and lower employee loyalty to the company resulting in higher turnover. One additional downside to these employees not previously mentioned is that some states and countries could require the employee to pay double in taxes. Once for the location where they work and a second for the state or country of the company they work for.

Some countries show a high number of telecommuters. For instance, India is the highest country with telecommuters at over 55%. However, Canada, the United Kingdom, and the United States are low on using telecommuters, comparatively speaking. Canada has about 8%, and both the United Kingdom and the United States are at about 9% of employees who telecommute.

When looking for telecommuting jobs, there are positions posted in job listings, on-line job sites, and with specific companies who you may find use telecommuters. Some popular telecommuting fields include customer service and sales. Additionally, if you work in a job where you see that it can be done just as effectively through telecommuting, consider creating a proposal outlining the benefits to the company, detailing how it would benefit the company, and present it to the employer.

Some women have taken the approach that they apply for a full-time role, prove what they can do in this role and then request alternative working arrangements, such as working from home a certain number of days per week.

Other work-at-home ideas

Let's take a look at a couple more popular choices for working from home, namely franchises and business opportunities. The advantage of these two programs is that you don't have to start from ground zero when building up the business because many other people have already succeeded. Plus, as you will see, these programs are already tried and true with many being household names. The companies share their marketing and operating concepts with those who are accepted to franchise with them. Additionally, both offer opportunities in any number of fields and interests.

We will talk about a few other, possibly lesser-known work-at-home ideas in this section.

Franchises

One of the great perks about getting into a franchise is that you have a tried map to follow from others who have made the business work. In fact, it has been considered one of the most successful forms of work-at-home business with nearly 95% still operating after five years.

With a franchise, one of the reasons that it works so well is because the franchise wants you to work within their established system. Most franchisees are known companies, they want customers to be able to get a similar experience from any branch. So as you can imagine, there is a lot of training time involved, and franchises require a commitment period. There will be legal disclosures and clauses to adhere to. When you are done, you will have the rights to sell or represent the franchise's product or service.

With this comes to support, networking opportunities, and virtually everything else, you will need to have the business succeed. This, then, helps with women who are re-entering or starting out in the workforce, to have confidence in that they will succeed.

Besides the time commitment, there is usually a large up-front fee to get started as well as an ongoing royalty fee paid to the franchise. Investments may be anywhere from under $15,000 to over $300,000. Examples of lower-end-cost franchises are those that sell flowers, coffee, health and beauty products, and accounting services. Examples of higher-end-costs, over $300,000, include restaurants, express care medical offices, and childcare centers.

If you are interested in joining a franchise, be sure to check for a track record. See what their training program entails. Talk to others who are in the program. Look at their entry requirements. Usually, franchises require that the person must meet the start-up capital and be willing to commit to their respective program. Be sure you have the time to devote to the training before you invest the money and effort.

Generally, franchises don't require an applicant to have experience in a particular field to be accepted as a franchisee. The most popular types of franchises women invest in, according to Franchise Direct, a source for information on franchising internationally, is children's products, computer and internet, cleaning services, and vending franchises with the lowest being automotive.

More on online business

The United States has the most franchisers of any other country. People interested in franchising can talk to banks, the SBA, and other sources to get funding assistance to enter into the franchising industry. Some of the SBA approved franchises include fields in coaching, consulting, and child-related entities. Women show interest in franchises such as health food, fitness, early education, and clothing.

Australia offers over a thousand franchise opportunities. It has been estimated that nearly 70,000 people are involved in franchising in Australia.

In New Zealand, nearly 94% of the franchises are New Zealand based companies. Also, nearly 80,000 people are employed by franchising in the country.

The United Kingdom has shown an increase in franchise interest of over 3% in the past few years. Almost 400,000 people are employed in franchising opportunities. In the United Kingdom, one of the up-and-coming franchise opportunities involves the health food industry.

Business Opportunities

Business opportunities are existing systems though vary greatly from franchises. They rarely have strict systems that have to be followed because unlike franchises, business opportunities usually aren't attached to a known name. Similarly, there is rarely a royalty fee. The up-front costs are typically very small concerning franchises – some starting as low as $500. Additionally, there tends to be less training time involved, so more business opportunity owners can better choose their hours as full or part-time.

Business opportunities may be more often based from home than franchises though cover a wide range of business-type interests. Some examples of business opportunities include medical billing, insurance, sales, website businesses, catalog sales, businesses, and many more.

Social Media Marketing/Influencer

There is another type of work-at-home opportunity called network marketing. Because of the way these programs are usually set up, some types of networks have been given a bad name and may even be illegal in some countries.

Sometimes known as "pyramids" or "pyramid schemes," these are programs in which participants move up in levels by gaining people who would work below you. As each level gains more people, you move up in levels. Each level gets a part of the actual product sales.

The benefits of these programs are that there are no commitments and often very minimum start-up fees – usually just the cost of the first set of products. The person who recruited you to enter into the network has a vested interest in your success so is likely to offer support and training, as you would do for your people.

A downside to this type of program is that it often takes a while to see income (usually you need to be up to a few levels). Additionally, the majority of network opportunities are in sales, so if you are not sales oriented, this might not be a good fit.

Web-based Businesses

Whether you are computer savvy or not, starting a home-based web business could be one of the more economical ways of working from home. With computer knowledge, you could save yourself time and money and have a little more freedom in making changes to your website. If you aren't very knowledgeable about computer systems, there are still going to be some pieces that could be easily learned. Additionally, there are plenty of resources available; from professional agencies who can start and maintain the site through freelancers and college students looking for experience and side work. There are even computer programs which can do a lot of the work for you depending on what you want to do.

With a web-based business, you are essentially selling something through the pages and links on the site. So the possibilities are endless for what you can do with it. If you are interested in selling one, two, or a line of products, this is a good way to do it. Because the internet is world-wide, you have a wide audience to sell to. For many, it's a fun, simple, and easy way to earn money.

There are several ways to find items to sell. You could:

* Sell your own products or services.

* Become an affiliate with other sites and people to sell other people's products. As an affiliate, you make a percentage of the sale.

* Sell for others as an e-worker or an i-worker. Look for web-based jobs on the internet using these key terms to find these opportunities.

* Start a drop-shipping business.

This latter option, a drop-shipping business, is basically where you would sell products from a manufacturer or wholesaler. From your website (the most common way to do sales as well as places like eBay), you would take the orders, provide the information to the manufacturer or wholesaler, who would then fill and deliver the items. Any profit in the sale price, after the wholesaler's costs is yours.

The benefit of drop-shipping is that you don't have to actually have the inventory or make any up-front purchases on the products to sell them. Generally, when you choose a manufacturer or wholesaler to work with and choose the products you want to sell, the company will provide you product info and photos to post on your sales page.

Working for yourself

In these previous opportunities, a lot of the groundwork was done. However, the opportunities already exist, which could be a positive or negative depending on what you would like to do. So another viable option is to simply start your own business from the ground up.

When you operate your own business, you wear all of the hats. You are the owner, boss, and employee. You pay yourself, offer your own benefits, and earn your own reputation. You handle the problems and get the accolades. You design the business as you want it to be run and do the work it takes to reach each point in the process. In essence, it's your baby all the way.

Starting your own business

The idea of being your own boss, of working in a field you feel you will enjoy, of having flexibility in your schedule, and in having the ability to decide your own income level are just a few of the reasons why women opt to start their own business. There are a range of different sizes of businesses from a one-person operation to a few employees to an entire company. In the United States, it is estimated that there are as many as 910,000 women-owned businesses as of 2007. Canada has over 800,000 as of 2011. Australia notes 900,000 women-owned businesses. There are nearly 620,000 in the United Kingdom. And women made up 36% of the self-employed workers in New Zealand as of 2007.

Some of the steps involved

Obviously, the first step to starting your own business is to have a desire. From this desire will come an idea. From this idea will come the motivation and outline of the work to do to make it all happen.

When there is an idea, the next step is to do a lot of research on it. Some of what you will want to know include details about the market itself; look into your competition, identify a specific niche and how to reach it, and most importantly, decide what you will offer your market. People typically buy products and services based on what it will do for them – how it will solve their problem. So when you develop your product and/or service, do so from the perspective of how it will benefit the buyer.

In your research, look into local and state and even government regulations as they apply to things like zoning, taxes, and other rules which may apply to an at-home business. Areas may be different, so don't skip this step.

Need to get financed? There is a wide range of options. There are agencies such as the Small Business Association, government programs, investors, and even private grants available for women who want to start up a business. Checking into a bank loan is another option.

For most of these finance options, you will need to have a complete and detailed business plan; especially for investors and bank loans.

Basically, a business plan is a complete concept of your business from A to Z. Business networks, associations, and sites with grant and loan information will have outlines and sample templates for creating a business plan.

In general terms, a business plan will contain information about the company, all management and board members involved as applicable, information on the industry and competition, how your business will fit into the market, operation statements, a very detailed financial plan, and any extra material that may help your case. Even if you are just starting and haven't actually launched the business yet, you still need to develop the financial plan. As a proposed or new business, most of the information will likely be estimates.

Be sure, when you write the plan, that you write it to the particular audience. An audience may be different from an investor to a bank officer, so write the plan for that respective party. Then, if you self-fund or don't need much upfront money, you may still want to create a simple business plan just to help keep you on track throughout the process.

You will need to set up your office. This could include a desk, phone, computer, cabinets, and so forth. Have a designated area that is going to be used just like your workspace. Having this specific space does several things.

One, it presents the boundaries to you and others in the home that this is your work area – your job. And when you are inside of it, you are working.

Two, it gives a designated place to "commute" to and from.

You arrive at the beginning of the determined work time and leave at the end of the work time. Third, for those who will have clients come to the "office," the work area is the space designed and decorated to accommodate those clients. Finally, this space, as long as it is used strictly for work, may be able to be written off on taxes.

Speaking of taxes, you will need to determine what type of business you will be. For instance, a business can be a single entity or sole proprietorship. It can be other types as well, such as a Limited Liability Corporation (LLC), non-profit, a partnership, or a cooperative. Note that it is possible to start as one type and move to another over time.

When the business is ready to have clients, you may need to do some marketing. This can be anything from spreading your business around through word of mouth to taking out full-scale ads in trade magazines and newspapers. Marketing can include having an internet website for publishing articles on your business field and joining associations that may help spread the word.

Having a website nowadays is more than merely a suggestion; it's virtually a requirement like any other piece of office equipment. Besides getting your brand out there, and by out there, it means world-wide, people can get to know you in the virtual sense. Even if you want to stay small and local, a website can help by providing a forum for you to post articles, information, event dates, and offer a way to be contacted.

Marketing could include networking, such as going to area trade and business association meetings. It could include giving free talks. Giving webinars or teleseminars. Obviously, the marketing options are vast. There are dozens upon dozens of programs on the internet, books, and on-line courses on the topic of marketing. Any of them can help to develop a strong marketing program.

While you are looking into the online marketing courses, consider taking a basic bookkeeping course or two. Again, community colleges, the SBA, and other entities will also probably offer such classes. Because it is so important to keep good records of the businesses activities, taking a course may help with the most effective and efficient way of doing so. Besides having the records for yourself, you may need them for investors, taxes, and other situations.

Of course, you need to set up your work schedule. Working for yourself is like working at any other type of job in that the day begins, there is lunch, and when the day ends, you go home. Set your daily work schedule and stick to it. And when it's time to go home, do so.

Leave the office behind and enjoy the balance of your life with family, other pieces of your life, and so forth.

Depending on what you want to do for your business, there may be some additional steps involved beyond these. However, for most of the start-up businesses out there, these are the basic pieces.

Considerations in working for yourself

Working for yourself may seem like a bit of a challenge, especially if your prior experience has been working for someone else. There isn't someone giving you work orders or watching over your shoulder per se. All of it is on you, not just to create the work that needs to be done, but to do it.

Everyone wants their business to succeed. For some, especially people just starting out in the self-employment arena, they think that the more time they put in, the more chance there is of success. However, in the majority of cases, it's truer to say that the more organized, disciplined, and efficient with the use of time one is, the better chance of success. Probably even more important is being balanced in terms of work and life. This creates a healthy business owner, and that virtually always guarantees success – in life as well as work!

Regarding work itself, be sure to prioritize tasks based on importance and urgency. Then try to get those items done first over the less urgent items to not get behind and have to play catch-up at the end of the day.

What about your appearance? Mark Twain said that "clothes make the man" or in this case, "the woman." Why this matters to someone who works out of home is because many sources suggest that what you wear affects your attitude. Some people joke that working out of home means getting to work in their pajamas. While there is some literal truth to this, for the professional person, part of the workday is getting ready, getting dressed, having breakfast, and going to work. It's no different for working at home.

As we just mentioned, working for yourself means being your own boss. Everyone who has ever had a job may have had a boss whom they disliked as well as some they might have liked – or at least appreciated some traits of. From this, when you are wearing the "boss" hat, be the boss you always wanted to work for both to yourself and to any contractors or employees you may have.

There are many benefits to working for yourself. There is a sense of satisfaction that comes with building a business from the ground-up and running it the way you believe it should be run. While you will put yourself into it, remember that like any other job, it is a part of you, though not all of you. You likely went into it so you could spend time with your family and do other things that matter in your life. Be sure to carry that forward and actually do those things daily.

Gaining Self-Confidence

Knowledge and motivation are definitely two important parts of the process of entering or re-entering the working world. Not just in the challenges of finding a job but in making the transition. There is another valuable piece that will be beneficial to your journey: confidence.

Confidence is basically defined as believing in the path you are taking. Further, it believes that you can succeed in your abilities to travel that path and reach your goal.

Add to this the idea of self-confidence, which is often defined as knowing that you can achieve your goal but doing so by letting go of the negative thoughts, doubts, and the outcome.

It is interesting to consider the concept of letting go of the outcome. Here you are, wanting to have a job, putting in the effort, the time, and the energy of trying to get a job and being told that you need to let go of the outcome of whether you will get that position or not. For as strange as it seems, it is actually a beneficial concept if you think about it.

Holding on to the outcome is like having tunnel vision. The truth of the matters is that you will likely have to apply for several jobs before getting that first interview. If you are focused on just one job, bent on getting it and holding on to only having that one job, you are likely setting yourself up for disappointment; especially if you don't get it for some reason. Further, you are probably not going to be motivated to fill out other applications, won't be open to other options, and so forth. Without getting into a job position, you won't be able to make the eventual run for the position you want to in respect to your ultimate goal. So letting go of the outcome helps you to stay focused on the bigger picture of finding a job and, at some point, move up to the position you subsequently desire.

Having tunnel vision keeps you from being, open to potential options. Realizing that there is more than one way to reach your goal may provide some interesting and otherwise unforeseen opportunities that could actually open up doors to possibilities that could be exciting and fulfilling. So staying open to options is important to the process.

Rarely does life offer the perfect path the way you wish it would be. A straight line to the desired goal with maybe a few steps to reach it. No, often it happens that it will take many steps and a few twists and turns to reach that desired endpoint. But those steps are great learning opportunities which only improve your confidence as you traverse the path and find success in step after step.

As we discussed earlier, it can take up to two years or more to find a job in some fields. So having the knowledge and staying motivated are valuable as well as having the confidence that you will find that job, even if it takes some time.

Developing confidence

What is great about confidence is that it is learned which means that anyone at any time can develop it. There are several ways to do this, and here are just a few of them.

Recognize that you don't have to do it alone

Pull out that list you made earlier of people who would support you. That list, right there, is a great example of how you are not alone. Having support on this or any path is invaluable. Others can be there to listen, boost your spirits up on those tough days or after a disappointment, and offer suggestions you may not have thought about. People can be there to share the triumphs and successes and cheer you on when you pass a major or minor milestone or when you reach your goal!

One of the keys to making the goal is to not stay stuck long after a down moment. Using your resources and letting others help can reinforce to you that you can, in fact, do it!

Another method for realizing you don't have to do it all alone is to find a group or create a group where people in similar situations can support each other and share successes. Often, support from people who are going through the same things, as well as being a part of a group, is very beneficial to any process.

Accept that you are human

As a mother, sometimes it seems like you have to be everything at all times. Truth is, you can't be everything. You are human. So when you are looking to have confidence, and you see a weakness in yourself, it puts a chink in that superhuman armor.

We all have strengths and weaknesses. We can use our strengths all of the time as a fuel to propel us through a variety of situations. And having the ability to accept that we aren't as adept in some areas as others is a valuable asset. In some instances, it's just a matter of learning to strengthen a weakness. In other instances, it's merely a weakness.

Here's another piece of good news: perfection – it doesn't exist. How freeing this is because for those who are "perfectionists," you can save yourself a lot of frustration, anger, and disappointment. In accepting that we, as humans, can always improve and move in the forward direction toward our goal but never reach it "perfectly" is a huge relief. As many may have already experienced, trying to reach, let alone maintain perfection, especially since it doesn't exist, is a real energy drain.

Mistakes happen: keep moving

Mistakes are simply learning opportunities. Amazing things have come from a mistake. For example, did you know that Formula 409, the cleaning product, was named for the number of times they tried to make the product and failed? It was on the 409th try that it succeeded! Just this example in itself shows well the reason to keep trying.

Sometimes, people feel they need to impose self-punishment if they make a mistake. Perhaps it was the inventor Thomas Edison who described it best when he was asked by a reporter about failing with the light bulb (it has been estimated that he tried somewhere between 6,000 and 10,000 times), Edison responded that he hadn't failed, not even once, but that he simply found many ways not to create the light bulb. So when you consider that you made an error, realize that you now know one way in which not to create that something!

Celebrate successes

We are often quick to point out our errors, but we have to learn to be quick in recognizing our successes! Each success we achieve is what we can build the next one upon. During those times when we feel that we can't succeed at all, we will have a trail in place that we can actually see, furthering us to say that "I did do this" and "I did do that." Hold these victories. You earned them, and indeed, they are valuable!

A good habit to get into, especially because feelings of success tend to be fleeting, is to write them down. If you are keeping a progress journal or any kind of written form of the progress and actions you are making in finding the job, be sure to note the successes. Highlight them with a marker or write them in different colored ink. Be sure to review them often to keep that attitude of succeeding in the front of your mind.

Similarly, when you receive a compliment, whether from a friend, relative, interviewer, or anyone, accept it, be grateful for it, and note it. Add it to your list or journal so you can refer to it and internalize its positive power as well.

Some additional points

Here are a few more quick points to keep in mind to help with gaining confidence:

* Don't focus just on the job. Have balance in your life, including time for family, work, school, exercise, fun, faith, and so forth.

* Now and then, do something out of the ordinary and against the typical pattern. For instance, if your daily routine is always the same, do one thing different. If you take the same route to the grocery every day, drive a different route. Start from the opposite end of the store than usual. Do something every day to keep the day out of the mundane.

* Check in with yourself often to be sure you are on track for your goal.

* Trust that you know that you are capable of doing things. Also, listen to your gut – it's an amazing guide.

* Let others help, whether it's people giving assistance with babysitting or a spouse helping with housework or a friend offering to drive that day or whatever it may be.

Tools of a confident person

Because confidence is something that can be learned, there are some valuable tools which you can acquire to assist yourself on the journey of gaining and maintaining confidence. The more tools you give yourself, the more opportunities you have to add confidence-building examples to your list.

Here are some aspects that you may want to try to have in your personal repertoire as you process through the journey.

Stay on task

There are going to be ups and downs, distractions, and other such interruptions along the path as you look for work as well as seek balance in your home and work life. There will be times you feel like you want to quit, want to change your whole plan, feel that you can't do it, and any number of reactions and emotions. These are all common.

Any goal worth having will provide this array of reactions and responses. Steps aren't always simple. Some will be while others will challenge you just a little bit beyond your comfort zone.

The key to it all, though, is to eventually get back on the path – to stay on task. Eventually, you will find that you can do this faster and easier after each time you get frustrated or disappointed.

Know that you can do it

Having faith in yourself, in your abilities, and in your desire to reach that goal is important as well as empowering. As we talked about earlier in this chapter, one way to add this type of confidence to your list is by looking back at your inventory of traits, skills, and experiences in addition to keeping a list of successes and compliments. All of this will help you to see and know that, in fact, you can and ultimately can achieve what you are setting out to do in some capacity.

Patience

With the generally rather long time-line involved in finding a job, it is easy to get impatient with the appearance of a lack of results. Plenty of questions will fill your thoughts about why you didn't get a job that you were so right for or why it's taking so darned long to even get an interview. But the facts are that you can't know the reasons for any of it. What you can do, however, is keep putting in the effort, keep believing in yourself, and know that eventually, it will happen.

Part of having a lack of patience is related to holding an expectation. It doesn't matter your background, experience, or really, any other factor. What matters is letting go of the belief that things should happen a certain way and only that way.

Confidence comes as you continue working toward your goal and knowing that the outcome will eventually arrive. That is part of why each small piece of the whole that you achieve is another step in that direction.

Choose your battles

Again, you likely won't know why you weren't selected for a job, and you may not be able to find out. But to take it personally, try to argue, or make assumptions or judgments about yourself deplete you of your energy and confidence. The journey will be filled with tests, only some of which will be worth fighting. Others will simply be irritations and distractions. So pick your battles carefully because you will want to save your energy for the ones that really can make a difference toward your end goal.

Other traits

A few other traits that will help contribute to your confidence level include:

* Being open to options and opportunities.

* Having a sense of humor rather than taking everything too seriously.

* Putting in the effort and time to making your goal a reality.

* Giving yourself a pat-on-the-back for each success.

* Being yourself and recognizing that you are a valuable asset.

* Accepting yourself and being compassionate to yourself regardless of what is going on inside or outside.

* Avoiding people that bring you down or tell you that you won't make it.

* Trying continuously to improve your skills.

* Taking care of yourself.

A few advanced skills

For women who were previously in management or supervisory roles, they may have a few additional skills to help them with having and gaining confidence. Some of these might include:

* Staying relaxed in stressful situations. As a supervisor, there were no doubt times when a cool head prevailed. Similarly, looking for work and balancing work and home may fall under a category where staying relaxed is a benefit. In many situations, this means staying to the facts of the situation rather than reacting emotionally to them.

* Staying focused. It is easy to get distracted and add issues to the mounting pile of stuff to do. Yet staying focused on the task itself, on the step you are working on, and on the goal will help to keep energy and effort flowing in the right direction.

* Taking the confidence forward. Managers need to be confident in their jobs. They need to show their subordinates that they can be supportive, handle problems, and provide solutions. They trust themselves and what they know as well as have the willingness to accept what they don't know with the awareness that they can find out.

Their goals on the job are often to bring the best out of their subordinates and can bring this forward for themselves as well.

Ways to network

This topic is about overcoming your apprehension about networking. For many people, the idea of going to meet a group of strangers, even if it's based on similar interest, is difficult. What do you say? How do you say it? How do you network and mingle?

Obviously, the best factor you have to come into the meeting with is the fact that you have a common interest with the other participants. As you consider going to the meeting, take it step-by-step. In other words, the first step is getting there. The second step is entering the meeting room. The third step is, and so forth.

Often, when you arrive at a meeting room, people will be gathered in small groups. Scan the groups to look for a familiar face. It's a good way to start. Often, if you are new, someone will notice. Usually, one of the officers or the recruiting member. They will typically come up to welcome you, which is a pleasant ice breaker.

Your goal isn't to talk to every person at your first meeting. Rather, a good goal is to talk to a few people, get familiar with the meeting process, and get comfortable with it. You want to step out of your comfort zone piece by piece. On subsequent meetings, besides talking to those you have already met, make a personal goal of talking to at least one new person each time.

If you are somewhat outgoing, consider putting on a name-tag to identify yourself, which will probably draw people to you. Bring a notepad so you can share names, numbers, and emails with the people you meet.

Typically there will be a period of introduction early on during the meeting. Have a few lines prepared, including your name, experience, and a blurb about your family. This way, you won't feel caught off guard.

If you find after mingling that you are comfortable in this group, consider doing some volunteering with them. Many groups have multiple opportunities for inter-group and outside group opportunities.

Avoid having the expectation that you will instantly find a job by going to a meeting. Additionally, avoid coming to the meeting with any kind of judgment or attitude that you won't find out any beneficial information or that because you were a manager at one point in the field, you won't be able to relate with the people there. This is a great learning opportunity, so it's best to go with an open mind.

Networking is a mutually beneficial experience. Not only can you meet others and get information on the field, but you can help others as well. Besides the volunteering opportunity, you can share your experience, offer support, and add to the numbers of the association which benefits everyone in it.

Checklist

Here are some valuable checkpoints to consider for confidence and networking:

Confidence

* Pull out your lists on skills, experience, and interests.

* Pull out your list of mentors.

* Look for support groups.

* Acknowledge your strengths and weaknesses (feel free to make lists if you are so inclined).

* Acknowledge your successes (make a list of many successes you have had in your life).

* Do something out of the ordinary daily.

* Check in with yourself to be sure you are on track with your goal.

* Stuck? Did you reach out to your support group?

* Let others help.

* Take care of yourself.

* Act as-if.

* Face your fears (make a list of fears you have overcome).

Networking

* Find associations or clubs related to your field of interest.

* Look for blogs, on-line groups associated with your field.

* Check with friends on Facebook and LinkedIn related to your field.

* Subscribe to publications in print or online in your field.

* Attend a local meeting.

* Set a personal goal as to how many new people you will meet each meeting.

* Volunteer at something in the association.

* Share your knowledge with others.

What to wear in the workplace

What you choose to wear in the workplace says a lot about you and does a lot for you. Have you ever noticed that when you are wearing casual clothing, you feel relaxed? Have you compared that to wearing a formal suit or Sunday clothes? You feel different, don't you? Well, that feeling can carry over into the job and your confidence.

If you are a manager or company executive, dressing up is usually expected. Plus, it gives the image of assurance and the perception of ability. It shows respect and confidence to the audience you are dealing with. It's as much an inward process as an outward one.

Perhaps you have seen people or had managers who dress up and who dress down. Do you tend to feel differently about these two people? In most situations, it's difficult to see these people with the same level of confidence, isn't it?

In many situations, the company will give you an idea of a dress code. What the company wants its employees to wear, be it a uniform or the classification of the dress. These may include a variety of levels of professional attire as we will discuss.

A little about what clothes say about you

Have you ever had the experience of staring in the mirror at your ensemble and feeling that something was missing? Just changing a simple piece like a belt or piece of jewelry changed the entire mood of the wardrobe and your demeanor. There are other aspects of your wardrobe that say something about you.

Often, when we dress, we consider what we will be doing on the job that day, who we may be seeing, and how we want to present ourselves. All of these can have an impact on what we take off the hanger. In exchange, our wardrobe can have an effect on us. Dressing up in formal attire can get a different reaction and response than would jeans and a t-shirt.

What you wear may have an effect on and represent your mood that day. Black, for instance, represents authority, is slimming, and is versatile in any workplace.

White is similarly authoritarian and versatile and indicates focus.

Blue is seen as conservative and subdued.

Brown is about being reliable and trusting.

Pink is often related to being emotional.

Yellow tells others that you aren't in a happy place that day.

Gray is worn when you want to just blend into the woodwork.

Red is more bold and flirty and considered a power color for women in high-level positions.

As a woman in management, avoid pastel colors as they tend to represent youth rather than experience.

For those who wear uniforms on the job, there is a blend of reactions from pride and feeling a part of the company to losing one's individuality. For others, it's a benefit to not having to invest in work clothes. So the range of how people see themselves and their clothes can be affected by personality and individually, as well.

Dressing for the workplace

Some workplaces have become more relaxed with their attire while others have structured company-wide dress codes. Through a dress code, a company may dictate the type of clothes considered acceptable in that workplace. This could include things like minimum lengths, and general types of clothing that it feels is appropriate for the image it wants to create inside and outside the company's walls.

Whether a company has a policy or not, use good judgment. Consider your environment and choose to wear an outfit that is possibly business casual, as opposed to street casual. We will define these terms shortly to help illustrate the differences.

Dress for your audience

When you send a company email to your peers versus management or your subordinates or clients, you are speaking to different audiences. Similarly, you would want to dress for them. If you are having a meeting with peers, dress for peers. If you are meeting a client, dress for the client. These are your audiences.

Dressing for your audiences has additional effects as well. For instance, it can affect your morale on the job. If you are in a field where you deal with a lot of clients and need to be dressing business casual or even formal yet you choose to wear street clothes, this plays on you in many respects.

For one, it sets you apart from your peers. If they are wearing business casual and you stand out in jeans, you will likely be the one seen as unprofessional and clients may prefer to work with others in your company. It could be telling the client that you aren't serious about their business or that you don't respect the company you work for or perhaps yourself for that matter. It can show a lack of confidence or simply say you can't be bothered.

Wearing appropriate attire, or at least something comparable with your peers helps you to fit into the group and can give you the confidence you need to compete in your job. It keeps you motivated and a part of the company mission. And you can reflect all of that upon the client in an effective manner through your appearance.

What is inappropriate?

Really, in most situations, what is appropriate or inappropriate could be considered a judgment call. This call can come from many sources, including HR, your supervisor, clients, or others in the workplace. It could come to you through words or non-verbally.

It's good to realize that what might be acceptable for someone to wear, such as a short skirt, maybe inappropriate for someone else. If you see someone wearing a short skirt at work, and consider doing so yourself, look at the situation rationally. For instance, if you put on a short skirt and it appears tight or when you sit or bend, you show your undergarments or even a bit too much flesh, it might not be considered appropriate for the workplace.

Showing cleavage, wearing tight clothes, and things like this may be considered appropriate for environments outside of work, such as a date, a casual evening with friends, or other such environments. In the workplace, though, it's about common sense and being somewhat conservative as a general rule of thumb.

Chances are you will hear something from your supervisor or HR if you are causing any kind of distraction in the workplace with your attire.

Non-verbal methods you might consider as potentially being disruptive are whistles and elevator eyes.

The bottom line is that you want to be taken seriously for your skills and talents in the workplace and not necessarily for your body and sensuality. And as a younger person or someone new to the workforce, you may not realize the actual effects your clothing has on how people see and perceive you. Consider how you want to be perceived by your co-workers and others up the ladder, especially if you have aspirations of moving up someday.

If you do end up being called on about your attire at some point, be professional about the feedback. If the issue requires clarification, such as confusion about a policy, talk to HR or your supervisor about it further. However, if your supervisor comments and suggests that you may not wear that specific type of clothing, you may want to listen. More than policy, what you wear has to do with professionalism. If you have a goal of eventually moving up in the company, your supervisor's comments may help you now with becoming more appropriate in your wardrobe for your goals.

If you aren't sure about the best clothes to wear in a particular environment, a great way to find out is to look at others in that setting and see how they dress. If you are starting out in the level of management and aren't sure, besides looking at others, consider the managers you have had. Which ones seemed more confident and epitomized the type of manager you want to be? Do you remember how they dressed? That would be a great pattern to follow; copying the type of manager you want to be!

This can apply to any job situation at any rank, from entry-level employee to management to upper-level managers to field workers and so forth. There is appropriate and inappropriate attire at any level. Return to the state of common sense and the idea of how you want others to perceive you and move forward from there.

Other situations

Some workers are issued uniforms by the company they work for, perhaps due to the nature of the job or to have its employees advertising the company logo. It is estimated that from 20-26% of companies internationally have their employees wear standardized uniforms including about 22% in the United States, 25% in Canada, 28% in the United Kingdom, and 38% in Australia. This could include just a shirt or a shirt and pants.

Additionally, depending on the job, some employers may allow casual dress such as jeans and t-shirts on an ongoing or limited basis. This is known as streetwear or informal dress. But on days when important clients or company executives are going to be at the site, it is inadvisable to wear street clothes.

Additionally, depending on what job you have, you may be required to wear additional items such as safety glasses, steel-toed shoes, or boots. This is often the case for people who work in blue-collar jobs or out in the field where possible hazards exist.

The difference between business casual and formal

Perhaps the greatest confusion comes in deciphering between the terms business casual and formal business dress. So if you aren't sure about the differences, you aren't alone.

Some of the definition depends on the business you work in and your rank in the company. Some are decided by company dress codes and subject to individual interpretation. The following guidelines may help in identifying some of the differences in these dress categories.

Business formal

Basically all about business suits. The clothes should be tailored with either slacks or skirts. The suits are often solid colors including black, blue, gray, and sometimes soft colors such as green, red, or pink; but not pastel. Business suits may have pinstripes.

Skirts should be no shorter than the knee and be worn with a slip. Besides, all formalwear should include hosiery and close-toed shoes. Makeup and jewelry are conservative.

Slacks or skirts should be pressed. Blouses should be buttoned and avoid showing excessive cleavage. Jackets should be fully buttoned and worn throughout the day.

The key to business formal is to think of as the classic business look rather than being trendy.

Business casual

In truth, the idea of business casual is a very gray area for most businesses. It is probably the main aspect of the confusion for the idea of business dress. The grayness of this level of the dress has pretty much spurred a lot of companies to enact a type of dress code, usually outlining what is generally acceptable attire for the workplace and more so, what isn't.

Notice the keyword in the definition above general. This implies that there is a lot of broadness and flexibility in the interpretation of what is acceptable. These dress codes may include guidelines for both men and women and could be subject to change with the evolving trends in clothing.

Usually with business casual, also called relaxed business attire, you will find things like jeans, shorts, tank tops, sundresses, tennis shoes or flip-flops, t-shirts, limits on necklines, skirt lengths, and so forth on the list of what not to wear.

What may be included in business causal are established lengths of skirts and dressy capris, sweaters, blouses, dresses, and some knits. While business formal included darker solid colors with coordinated skirts/slacks and blouses and jacket, casual offers more flexibility. Colors tend to be patterned as well as solid, not as strict on the color, and more relaxed with coordination. While there is usually a jacket, it can be buttoned with one or two buttons rather than completely, and it is appropriate to remove it during the workday. In business casual, make-up is still conservative as is jewelry. Shoes are flat or low heeled.

Smart casual

Let's throw another term in here, smart casual. This term is less formal than business casual but refers to more specific attire such as slacks, blouses, vest, knits, and a simple jacket. Shoes might include boots, flats, or low heels. Jewelry is still kept to simple, complementary items.

This level could include coordinated turtlenecks and dressy jeans. Some define it as a bit of a sportier business casual – minus the track shoes.

Nearly a third of companies allow for smart casual attire including an estimated 37% of companies in the United States, 43% in the United Kingdom, 35% in Canada, and 40% in Australia.

The difference in business casual and smart casual is mostly in acceptance. The term smart casual came from the newer working generation and allows for a more relaxed atmosphere in the workplace as a whole. Business casual is often considered more traditional and a bit more tailored.

Casual Fridays

Some companies allow for days when you may be allowed to wear jeans and a nice knit to work. The most common such situation is known as casual Fridays; a concept that is found in companies internationally. On these days, still, keep in mind that you are at the workplace. Be sure that the jeans are without holes or stains, fit appropriately, and are still tasteful.

In Australia, smart casual includes tailored pants and tops with minimum accessories. Often if companies aren't requiring uniforms, smart casual is the most common type of workplace attire. New Zealand, the United States, and Canada are seeing an increase in a more casual workplace attire. The United Kingdom, depending on the career field, is seeing slightly more companies still with formal attire.

It is interesting to note that employees, in general, recognize a variance in productivity related to the level of dress worn on the job. For instance, an estimated 70% of employees in Australia felt that they were more productive when they wore professional clothing on the job over casual clothes. It's fairly level in the United States (45% formal to 55% casual) and in Canada (52% formal to 48% casual). In the United Kingdom, about 63% of employees felt more productive in formal attire with about 37% feel they functioned better in casual dress. It is also interesting to note that nearly 40% of workers believed that those who typically dressed casually were not likely to move up into management positions. Over 65% of employees believed that managers should be dressed more formally than their subordinates.

A few more situations

When it comes to how to present yourself in any sort of job situation, there are usually going to be questioned. Here are a few additional job-related situations you might run into and some suggestions on how to best present yourself in terms of your attire.

Dressing for the interview

It is estimated that appearance is given as much as 73% of the consideration by a potential employer. So how you present yourself really does matter.

Typically, the idea is to approach the interview as if you were already on the job. If this is the case, dress like those already in the position you are interviewing for.

For example, if you are interviewing for a blue-collar type job, wearing street casual or even smart casual may be all you need. Chances are good you will be issued a uniform in the job if you were to get it.

If you are going for a corporate position, obviously business formal is more appropriate. Remember to dress for your audience. If you aren't familiar with the attire of the field, ask others you know who might be in the work field. Or, consider calling the front desk of the company where you will be interviewing and ask what the typical attire is for the position you are interviewing for.

In any case, keep the makeup and jewelry to a conservative level unless you are trying for a job where makeup and jewelry are part of what you will be doing. Avoid torn, stained, or wrinkled clothing and clothes that draw attention away from your qualifications for the job.

Again, unless the job you are applying for specifically relates to things like excessive piercings, unique haircuts or styles, or clothing such as torn jeans, pants that hang down to your knees, tight shirts, and the like, avoid these situations. Commonly, these are not what potential employers are interested in seeing. When an employer looks to hire people for the company, they consider how the person may relate to the company's customers and clients, their bread, and butter.

So if you are looking at a job in the piercing industry and have a lot of them yourself, great, you may be a perfect fit! If not, and you are trying for a job in some other field, then piercings may not put across the right air for the company. So before going to the interview, or possibly even applying for the job, ask yourself if you want a job where you may change your appearance, tone down some aspects of yourself to fit the job, or even dress up to meet the company's expectation. If it's something you feel you can and want to do, then apply. If not, then move on to the next opportunity and save time and effort.

Dress for networking

When you are preparing to go to a networking event, as a member, you want to present a confident image. Many organizations will tell you what the attire is for that meeting – usually business casual. And especially if you are going to a network to find a job, it is always a good idea to put out a great impression. Secondarily, following the group's dress code helps to feel a part of the group.

Dress for company functions

There are times when the company sponsors a picnic or other function and invites all of its employees and staff to attend. The key concept to keep in mind is that it is a company function.

For formal events, obviously, it's best to wear formal attire. For casual events, it's better to tone down but to remain tasteful. Avoid things like tank tops, short shorts, excessive cleavage, excessive makeup, and so forth.

In addition to clothes, also watch your attitude and behavior. Although you may not be directly on workplace grounds, you are still in the presence of company employees. It's best to avoid gossip and slander. Don't drink alcohol to excess. Be conservative. Again, it's still a work function, and your behavior may well be noted.

Dress for your own business

For the self-employed, the fundamental rules are the same – dress for your audience and how you want them to perceive you. Additionally, dress for yourself in whatever attire gives you confidence each day on the job. Even if you aren't meeting a client in person but are talking with him or her on the phone, your attitude shines through. It does depend on your field. Obviously, if you are someone who works out in the elements a lot rather than attending meetings, your level of dress may be much different.

Summary of dressing for the job

The key concept to keep in mind about the psychology of what you wear has to do with basically two aspects:

* How you feel when you are on the job

* How others perceive you.

This key helps you to decide daily, what you want to wear on the job with or even beyond the company dress code.

Many women, whether working in a blue-collar job with a uniform or wearing solid, dark-colored suits, worry that they aren't dressing "feminine" enough. Women can be and are feminine beyond their clothing. They don't need to dress down or risqué to prove that. It's about believing and realizing that you are powerful as a woman first and the clothes merely reflect that on the outside – no matter what you are wearing!

Finally, another point to keep in mind is that even if you have worked in the same career field for some time, different companies may have slightly different dress codes. It could be based on the type of clients they work with or simply the management's perspective. Be sure to not assume that if you change to a different company, the code will be the same. Check with your supervisor or HR if you have questions.

Checklist

The checklist for this section is a little bit different. It involves considering your wardrobe as well as the psychology behind it.

* Decide what level of attire you are willing to consider working with and apply for positions that meet this level.

* Decide what image you want to project to clients and co-workers.

* Match your wardrobe to that image daily.

* Look at your wardrobe. Take a detailed inventory.

* What level, based on this chapter, does your wardrobe fit into? Do you need to update or add any pieces to what you already have?

* As you look over your inventory, have you changed? Are there some pieces that are outdated for who you are today? If so, make those changes to reflect who you are now.

Supporting yourself

This chapter is devoted to talking about ways to support the important and invaluable topic of you.

Ways to support yourself

It is amazingly easy to fill up the day with errands, work, all the to do's and a whole lot of other things that you feel compelled to get done. However, somewhere in the racing around, as the sun sets and it's suddenly bedtime, you realized that you didn't have the chance to do something for yourself. You may find it's okay for a day or two. But then you begin to get tired, a little on edge, and eventually, maybe even a little depressed.

The process of integrating home and work involves the inclusion of many factors, preferably per day. There is work, there is family, there are chores, and there is you. If you think about it for just a simple moment, without you, most of the rest doesn't quite flow right. So you need to take care of you so that work, family, and all of the rest, can function at its best!

Let's discuss a few ways that you can do this:

Exercise

Taking care of yourself includes taking care of your body. Exercise helps with so many parts of the whole such as the physical body itself, stress, emotions, psychology, and overall well-being. It gets your heart rate up in a healthy way, motivates you to drink water which flushes toxins, helps to clear the mind, and gives you strength. But as a working mom, how can you make time to do any of it?

Like with most things you want to do for yourself as a career woman, you have to literally set aside the time. If time is tight, consider doing different types of exercise. For instance, instead of going to a gym where travel time is a factor, workout at home. There is a wide range of programs you can pop in that are on Youtube. Use an exercise machine. Get up early and walk or run in the neighborhood. Even video game machines offer gym-related programs.

Finding time could be about setting aside 15 or 30 minutes after the children go to sleep or after you finished taking care of the fur babies. Go right after work if it's convenient. Or go before work.

The benefits of exercising far outweigh the sacrifices. Working out even a few times a week is a benefit that shouldn't be denied.

Eat and sleep

This seems like a strange topic to be discussed, but if you look back on the last few days, what have you tended to give up first for lack of time? Breakfast or lunch? Sleep? Did you forget to make lunch and grab a candy bar from the machine at some point during the day, then returned to work instead of taking a full break?

Once time starts to crunch, anything related to you tends to go first, doesn't it? – including the basics of food and sleep.

Your body runs on fuel. Things like stress, not eating, and overworking can attack it. This is why even something as simple as the basics is so imperative. Eating balanced meals, drinking plenty of water, and getting enough sleep daily are fundamentals which if ignored, can and likely will eventually have an effect on every part of your being.

Similarly, when you need more time to finish something or to get going on the day, often it's sleep that goes by the wayside. A study of full-time working mothers showed that over 59% of them admitted that they didn't get enough sleep. Worry and family issues tended to keep most of them awake added to the lack of a consistent sleep schedule.

A lot of important things happen during sleep. You rest, rejuvenate, and important chemicals are released during this time. If you don't remember how ineffective you are without sleep, think about when you brought your child home as an infant and were up every few hours. How rested did you feel then? It's a good example of how sleep is important.

If you are having trouble sleeping, consider setting regular sleep schedules, doing relaxation or meditation before bed, and making the bedroom as comfortable a space as possible. Avoid drinking caffeine before bed, and try to find productive ways of dealing with daily stresses before you go to sleep.

A life of lists

Never mind diamonds, lists are a working mom's best friend. Lists are your most readily available, simplest tool. They can be used for everything from planning the week of meals to making the grocery run to what needs to be done that week to school events and so forth.

What is useful about having a list is that not only can you see what is coming or needs to be done, but you can also see what has already been completed. There is a sense of accomplishment with that. Too, you can get an idea of where and when you can fit in another item and make adjustments as needed.

Dealing with stress

Stress will happen, it comes with life. Stress is inevitable when you are trying to juggle your life and all of its parts. However, you can get more done and better enjoy the day if you are as realistic and calm as you can be during each circumstance. When you act and react out of stress, you tend to get less done, be more frustrated, and take more personally.

There are a variety of ways in which you can help yourself to ease the stress:

* Keep things simple. The more complicated and intricate something is, the more stressful it can become. This is why it is a good idea, for instance, to make a simple breakfast in the morning. Doing so keeps the flow of the morning moving and avoids potential issues from arising.

* Realize that if you don't have time to do something all the way through, get started on it and come back when you can. Five minutes of cleaning the kitchen is a start. You may have to return to finish, but some will be done. Too, it helps to bring slight relief to the worry that is no doubt going to arise over the kitchen and concern if you aren't able to complete the task all in one take.

* Similarly, if you aren't able to get to something that day or maybe even that week, give yourself a break. Things happen. You may get distracted, or something more immediate could appear. Invariably, something will get pushed aside. Remember, you can only do so much in a day.

* Like we just talked about, keep lists. This helps with time management and thus, lessen stress. Be sure to cross things off to recognize completion and give that sense of acquiring some open time. In conjunction with the last point, too, prioritize your lists in case you do need to put something off for a while.

* Be organized – keep things in familiar places. If you know you have to drop things off in several different locations, keep the items in one

place in the house or even in the car and drop them as you are in that area. Driving all over town is a huge time cruncher with traffic. So unless it's an important item, chances are good you will have an errand somewhere in the area during the week. If not, you could always make a family trek out of it for the weekend.

* Here's one that may sound odd but it works. Give something to someone. You may be thinking, I give my time to everyone all day. But in this instance, it's about giving accolades, gifts, and gratitude. The purpose of this is simple. You aren't able to be worried or stressed and grateful at the same time. So every chance you get, be grateful rather than stressed!

The biggest thing you can do for stress is to relax. This can mean taking time out for ten or fifteen minutes, take a walk, stop and meditate, or whatever helps you to gain internal calmness. This really helps when you had a tough workday and don't want to take it out on the family.

Fun

Fun is not just a three-letter word. It's an essential piece of life. When you work all day and come home to the family, do you take time to have fun as well? Fun can be anything from sitting with everyone for a family night event to going on a drive over the weekend to bowling a game to planting some flowers in the yard. Fun can be anything that gives you enjoyment. Life is about having fun, so even if you have to schedule fun in your day, be sure to have some!

A few more ideas

Here are a few reminders and ideas to close the chapter on taking care of you:

* Like we talked about in the last chapter, have a routine. This helps you, and everyone knows what to expect and catch things that might be out of alignment or need to be done.

* On your way to and from work, listen to relaxing, calming music.

* Make a list of things you enjoy doing and keep it handy. Plan some of these things into your week as you are able.

* Start and/or end your day with a few minutes of calm breathing or meditation.

* The day will offer a variety of stresses to add to the pile. Consider if they are worth holding on to or not, and if not, simply let them go.

Checklist

* Integrate exercise into your weekly routine. Schedule time if you need to.

* Make a lunch when you make the children' lunches to be sure and have a good meal. Consider having breakfast as well.

* Set a regular schedule for going to bed and make changes to it only as an exception, not a rule.

* Recognize and deal with stresses as they arise.

* Take ten to fifteen-minute time outs throughout the week.

Organizing yourself

We have spent a considerable amount of this book talking about ways to organize time. Let's face it, as a working woman, a woman looking for work, or even a full-time mother, time is a valuable commodity. In that light, this chapter will focus on additional ideas and ways to manage and organize aspects of your life.

The benefits of having an organizational system are abundant. Having a system in place helps to keep things in your life structure. A system allows you to include everyone in it – from the children and their events to your partner's schedule and anyone else who needs to be included. For example, if you are taking care of a parent, he or she may have appointments that need to be attended. Additionally, while not an immediate part of the family dynamic, if you know that your daycare provider will be unavailable for a week or two, you can have it on the schedule and make other arrangements.

Having a system can also help to keep everyone up on changes, additions, or subtractions to the schedule, and on ways to share responsibilities. If you find that two activities overlap, a formal system can provide a way to let each partner know the event and who is handling it.

It is a way to get things out of your head and down on paper so that you are free to think about other things. Since worry is a complex which interferes with sleep and contributes to stress, having thoughts down on paper helps to keep the worry out of the way.

Today, there are a wide variety of tools for organizing your life in everything from:

* On-line programs to old fashioned notebooks.

* Programs and apps for iPads and iPhones.

* A plethora of ways to utilize Microsoft Word and Excel in constructing calendars, lists, and other visual pages which can illustrate the daily, weekly, and even monthly plan. What's more, they are easy to print out and hang around the house or put in a binder.

* Bound organizers, which come in sizes from letter-size pages to a smaller size that can fit easily in your purse. They have many resources included, such as notepads, planners, phonebooks, and tabs to separate out the sections.

With so many options, there is bound to be a time-saving option which will benefit you and your family. We'll spend the rest of this chapter reviewing some valuable points and noting some additional ones. There are sure to be some methods which will assist you in getting even more organized than you may already be and have more time for other things in your life!

Integrating Techniques

Perhaps you have heard about the value of keeping things simple. Related to saving time and stress, it is truly a worthwhile concept. When tasks are kept simple, they are often more do-able, which leads to faster completion and a feeling of accomplishment. As things are completed, there is less anxiety and worry (about getting it done).

Simplicity has its place in the home as well as on the job. At home, keeping chores, schedules, routines, and expectations simple allow for them to be done with less hassle for everyone. The more complicated a task or chore, the more things can go awry, and the more time it could take to finish. The key, then, is to, whenever possible, keep things simple!

Establish a routine

In a routine, everyone knows what to expect – simply put, what, how, and when. It also keeps children aware and on a consistent system. This helps keep children healthy because structure gives them a sense of security and predictability. Besides, it helps you to be sure that everything gets done the way it needs to be done and provides a pretty easy way to identify if it isn't.

As you prepare to organize a routine, the key consideration is to decide what needs to be accomplished. Part of the routine equation is determining what needs to be done and about how long it will take to do it.

Let's demonstrate a sample weekday routine. We will assume that there are going to be basically two routines daily – specifically one in the morning and one in the evening. Here is what each may look like.

Morning

The morning scenario is likely to be about getting yourself ready for work and getting the children ready for school or daycare. This could include such pieces as getting dressed, brushing teeth, and eating breakfast.

* Getting yourself ready might include rising from bed, showering, getting dressed, maybe a few minutes of mediation or working out, grabbing a cup or two of coffee.

* Eventually it will be time to wake the children. Do they get their own clothes (which may be done the night before) or do you select it for them? While they brush their teeth, you might pick their clothes, and as

they dress, you could be preparing a quick, simple breakfast. If you don't have children, maybe you have to walk, feed, or bathe the dog.

Once the morning basics are covered, consider if any other factors will be included in the morning routine. Remember to allow time for these extras as well.

Consider how much can be done the night before (and moved into the "evening" routine)? For instance, get book bags and diaper bags ready the night before. If there is ironing to be done, add it to the evening routine. And be sure to always add "hugs" to the morning routine!

Several follow-up thoughts

Keeping schedules and routines are useful, but they need to be used and managed. You might find it trying at first when you are initially starting a routine. When you implement it with the basic design in mind, it will likely smooth out in a reasonable period. Allow the routine to form before re-assessing it and adding and subtracting items that may make the process flow better for you.

Another comment about forming a routine is to ensure consistency. So if you are, for instance, including family time, such as everyone being at the dinner table, in your routine, be sure not to allow exceptions too often. Part of maintaining a routine is to keep it regular and ongoing. Not only does allowing members to miss dinner too frequently interrupt the pattern for others in the household, but it's also easy to let it get out of hand.

If you are keeping an organizational system such as a planner or other form of keeping daily or weekly schedules, be sure to maintain it. For items that aren't regular items, erase or cross them off as they are completed. For lists, do the same so that you can see what has been completed and what still needs to be done. Doing this saves you from having to remember if you did it or not. Staying current helps to keep you well organized!

Additionally, I realize that there is a good chance that not everything on your list will be completed in the time frame that you allowed. Be sure to have a personal system in place to prioritize tasks so that the time-sensitive and important items are done with other, less urgent tasks able to be moved if they aren't done.

Of course, one way to help get things done is to delegate. As you do, mark it on your list or on the schedule with color coating or written note and let others see that the task will be completed by someone else.

This is where a dry-erase board would be useful for keeping track of routine points such as chores and schedules inside the home. Because it's a good idea to keep the schedule available for everyone to see, the board is a good way to do this. Additionally, it is easy to update, and there are multiple color pens to use with each person getting his or her own color. Again, be sure to keep the board updated regularly.

An additional useful tool for the morning and evening routine is to consider having a crate by the front door where anything leaving the next day will be placed. This way, if something is missing the night before, there is time to search for it instead of racing around in the morning where time is much more limited.

Hire a Personal assistant

For those busy working women who can use some additional hands, an option is to hire someone to do some of the time-consuming tasks. A personal assistant can provide a wide range of help. This is a great option if you are self-employed to have an assistant to run errands, as well as possibly help with tasks at the office.

As with anyone who you hire to help with aspects of your life, you want to be sure to take the time to do the reference checks and do an interview. Still, you want to get an idea of how you feel about the person because he or she could become something of a buffer for you in several aspects of your life.

Personal assistants can offer such services as transportation, coordinating, scheduling, managing, errands, grocery shopping, and meal preparation, house cleaning, data entry, bookkeeping, phone work, computer assistance, and more. So depending on what you would like to have assistance with, you could likely find someone to meet those needs.

Planning meals

For many career-oriented women, the greatest task is around planning and making meals. And throughout the book, we had touched on some ideas about this topic, including:

* Planning a week ahead so that the trip to the grocery is a once a week trek. Having a menu also helps to avoid buying a lot of extras, so you save both time and money.

* Looking online or in cookbooks for quick recipe ideas.

* Making double portions when you do cook, and freeze some for another time.

Planning meals isn't just about dinners but breakfasts and lunches during the week, as well as weekend meals. All of these should be included in the grocery list.

Another benefit to having a planned list is that it is a great way to guarantee that, at home anyway, your children are eating the way you would like them to. And of course, the planning of meals:

* Avoids that redundant question of what are we going to have for dinner? Posting the weekly meal schedule in the kitchen lets everyone know of the plan.

* Removes the stress that comes with nearly everything to do with meals.

It's a good idea to get everyone's input when considering meals.

Additional considerations around meals

Planning meals can include some outside influences. For instance, cutting coupons adds up to some savings for the family budget and can provide some satisfying meal ideas. When you get coupons, be sure to set them with your list immediately, so you don't have to search for them later.

Another way to save a few dollars is to consider the weekly sales in your area and use them as ideas. For instance, if the chicken is on sale, find a couple of chicken recipe ideas and stock up while the sale is on.

Additionally, don't be afraid of left-overs. Take them for lunches or freeze them for a later time.

Keeping on track with your weekly meal planning can really go a long way in saving time and stress. Like with any of the other time-saving ideas, this one needs to be used and maintained to see valuable results!

A few final ideas

Having a washing machine and dryer at the house can be a convenience. Remembering to fill it can be tiresome. If you find you are getting behind on laundry, consider going to a laundry facility and taking a couple of hours to catch up on all of the laundries at the same time. While your doing laundry read a book or watch some personal development videos, so your not having to miss out on crucial time.

Checklist

* Establish a system that works for you! – on your phone, in an organizer, etc.

* Establish a routine for morning and evening at home.

* Decide what needs to be accomplished in the morning and evening routine.

* Create a meal plan weekly.

* Make a grocery list for lunches, breakfasts, and dinners for the week.

* Have coupons ready.

* Have a list of resources available such as support groups and names and numbers of other working mothers to use as needed.

Prepare

Invest in Training

Once you have determined the direction of your ideal career path and how that fits into your life, your personality, and your skillset, some additional training may be necessary to refine your skills or acquire a new set. Your answers to the following questions will determine the amount of training you will need:

Your skill set – are you picking up a new skill or using a preexisting one?

Industry knowledge – are you in a new industry, or re-entering one that you are already familiar with?

How have the industry and your skillset evolved? E.g., most industries are undergoing a digital transformation – are you up to date?

How much time have you been away from the corporate world? Do you need to brush up your Excel and PowerPoint skills?

You can use the table below as a guideline for determining how much training you need.

New Industry, same function (limited training)	Same industry, same function (leas...
New Industry, new function (most training)	Same industry, new function (some...

Training will also be decided by your budget and your time. I advise relaunches to think of training as an investment – the more you do, the more valuable you become, and this translates into a higher salary and a shorter relaunch time. Each of the three web sites listed in P1 also has links to online courses. Also, most universities have online certificate programs. For example, MIT has a big data and a cybersecurity program, and there are government programs (e.g., the Small Business Administration offers a lot of classes in strategy, finance, marketing, technology, and new business).

Personalize

Take a Stand on your Personal Brand

What is your personal brand? Your brand helps you establish credibility in your field, break the stereotypes of a previous career when you relaunch into a different field, and position you for leadership roles.

Many factors can define your personal brands such as your previous expertise, the size and the quality of your network, and your values. I recommend also looking at the three websites in Chapter 1 for additional color. Here are some pointers as you think about your personal brand:

Identify the values that define you. Are you on the board of a company? Are you actively involved in your local community? What causes are you passionate about?

What are some of your proudest personal and professional achievements?

What do you want to be known for and get better at?

Develop a story of who you are that will inspire trust, familiarity, and credibility.

Develop your social media presence. Are you on LinkedIn? Which groups do you follow? Which posts do you comment on regularly? Are there any influencers you follow? Who are your role models? Invest in a good headshot. Seek recommendations on LinkedIn from your past colleagues.

Find a niche and become an expert in that area. Listen to podcasts. If you can write, start a blog.

Update your resume.

Set a rule for how quickly you will respond to emails. Proofread them before sending.

Join an employee group or a professional organization.

When I first relaunched into my own business after ten years in finance, my personal brand was as follows:

I am a founder of a high-quality children's clothing line that is made in New York City and sources woven cotton from East Africa. Promoting education and children is my passion, and hence, we contribute 5% of our proceeds to Scale Africa, a non-profit that builds schools and improves infrastructure in remote African villages.

Partner

Partner through Networking

Networking is important throughout your career – for new roles, to get tapped for the right projects that will propel you up professionally, to understand the company politics, to identify mentors and sponsors, and to keep abreast of industry trends in your field. Even after I returned to the corporate world, I continued to reconnect with old colleagues for coffee and lunch. Wharton professor and the author of [Give and Take: A Revolutionary Approach to Success,](#) **Adam Grant** notes that reconnecting with former classmates, former co-workers, and dormant connections can be more valuable than current connections because you are likely to have redundant knowledge and be in touch with the same people as your more current connections.

Here are some ideas that have worked for me:

My Top 20 Tips for Networking

Create a master networking list

Outline your career goal and be prepared

Spend 10-15 minutes communicating with one person a day

Set up informational interviews

Get in touch with old colleagues

Get in touch with your alumni and attend events

Offer to help or do something for the other person

Take them out for coffee

Listen more than you talk

Do some research about the other person

Find something in common: a hobby, TV show, etc.

Send a follow-up email

Ask them to introduce you to someone else and offer to do the same for them

Create an Excel spreadsheet that tracks all your conversations

Write down something unique about each person on the back of their business card

Post relevant articles on LinkedIn (I don't do this yet, I really should)

Follow key influencers and five companies

Join two or three LinkedIn groups and comment on posts (I follow way too many groups!)

Set a goal of meeting with one new person a week (if you are relaunching) or 2 people every month if you are just maintaining a network

Join an employee organization and an industry association

5 Icebreakers for Networking

What business are you in?

How did you get started in that role?

What do you like best about your role?

What keeps you up at night?

What advice do you have for someone like me who is trying to break into the industry?

Panel

Create a Panel of Advisors

According to the career advice website Landit, all of us should have a panel of advisors (referred to as a board of directors) that includes a mentor, a sponsor, a career coach, a close friend, and a connector.

A good mentor inspires you to see a possible future and then helps you to set goals to achieve it. He or she knows your strengths, can help you work through obstacles, can make career introductions, and keeps you on the path to your goals.

There are multiple stories of successful women who have had great mentors in their lives. For example, Ursula Burns, the former CEO of Xerox, had many mentors along the way. Ms. Burns started at the firm in 1980 as an engineering intern and rose to become CEO of the company in 2009. A mechanical engineer herself, some of her mentors included Wayland Hicks (a senior executive), former Xerox CEO Paul Allaire, and former Xerox CEO Anne Mulcahy. Not all your mentors need to have strong leadership positions, however.

Finding a great mentor requires work because it's a reciprocal relationship, and they must believe they will also gain something from the relationship. In fact, mentors grow from their relationships with their mentees and become better leaders. Ursula Burns spoke up about company policy to very senior professionals. This got her the attention of the CEO, who recognized her leadership potential. Also, Ms. Burns gained the respect and trust of senior management by taking on the management of business units and turning them around.

A mentor can be the following:

A peer or someone more experienced than you

A Trusted individual who is invested in you

At the same organization, or at a different one

Someone who helps you articulate your goals and stay accountable

An individual who has seen your potential and believes in you and your growth

A sponsor is someone who will put their reputation on the line for you, will support you when you are not in the room and will create opportunities for you. Sponsors can turbo-charge your career and do so because it will reap professional rewards for them. It takes time to find a good sponsor. A sponsor relationship is built on trust and requires discretion. This is especially important for professional women because it is still the case that women must go the extra mile.

Women and minorities often overlook the value of a sponsor.

In [(Forget a Mentor) Find a Sponsor, The New Way to Fast-Track Your Career](#), Sylvia Ann Hewlett notes that one should have three sponsors; one within the same department, a second in a different department, and a third outside the organization.

Some questions to ask when looking for a sponsor include:

Will the sponsor develop you as a leader?

Will the sponsor advocate for your promotion and create opportunities for you?

Does she or he work in a related field or have influencers in your field?

Is this someone for (or with) whom you have worked successfully in the past?

Does your professional success simultaneously propel their career?

Coaches

According to Landit, some of the items that coaches can help you with include:

Defining your goals or a new career

Excelling in your position

Executive presence

Unexpected obstacles

Enhancing confidence and a positive self-image

Leaving or starting a job

Management and leadership

In Creative Mentorship and Career Building Strategies, author Mary Pender Greene takes a different approach to build a panel of advisors based on the premise that you should go to multiple individuals for different types of expertise. Among others, the panel of advisors should include the following:

A chief marketing officer – to help with personal branding, brand identity, and niche marketing

A chief technology officer – to guide social media, your personal website, and blogging

A chief financial officer – to help you determine your compensation, evaluate job offers, benefits and retirement planning, and other investments

A chief legal officer who understands the legal issues and can help you negotiate contracts, provide advice on hiring and termination – crucial when you are starting a company

A chief political officer who understands office politics which can either enhance or impede your career.

Don't Go It Alone – Include a Fellow Mentor on Your Panel of Advisors

As a Mentor myself, I recommend it. Why? Because there are so many challenges unique to relaunches – it sometimes helps to get perspective from someone that has gone through a similar path.

www.ingramcontent.com/pod-product-compliance
Lightning Source LLC
Chambersburg PA
CBHW021825170526
45157CB00007B/2687